D1303542

ainsley harriott's meals in minutes

ainsley harriott's meals in minutes

Published by BBC Worldwide Limited
80 Wood Lane
London
W12 0TT

First published 1998
Reprinted 1998 (ten times), 1999
First published in paperback 1999
© Ainsley Harriott 1998
The moral right of the author has been asserted.

Recipes developed and written in association with Angela Nilsen and Vicky Musselman for
BBC Good Food Magazine and Silvana Franco.
Studio Photographs by Juliet Piddington © BBC
Location photographs by Craig Easton © BBC
Remaining studio photographs by Roger Stowell for *BBC Good Food Magazine* © Roger Stowell.

Commissioning Editor: Nicky Copeland
Editors: Kate Quarry and Rachel Brown
Art Editor: Jane Coney
Design by Town Group Creative
Home Economist for Juliet Piddington: Sarah Ramsbottom
Home Economists for Roger Stowell: Vicky Musselman and Angela Nilsen

DORLING KINDERSLEY PUBLISHING, INC.
www.dk.com
Publisher: Sean Moore
Editors: Chuck Wills, Gary Werner

First American Edition, 2000
10 9 8 7 6 5 4 3 2 1
Published in the United States by Dorling Kindersley Publishing, Inc.
95 Madison Avenue, New York, New York 10016

ISBN 0-7894-6726-7

Set in Trade Gothic Condensed and Franklin Gothic by Town Group Creative.
Printed and bound in Great Britain by Butler and Tanner Ltd, Frome.
Color origination by Radstock Reproductions Ltd, Midsomer Norton.
Jacket printed by Lawrence Allen Ltd, Weston-super-Mare.

All eggs used in the recipes are medium size.
All vegetables except new potatoes should be peeled unless the recipe says otherwise.

contents

Believe me, once you get into *Meals in Minutes* your enthusiasm for good, simple nosh becomes more and more infectious. You'll be able to bounce into your kitchen knowing that whatever is hanging around can be quickly whipped into a gourmet feast. Food shopping will be done with confidence invaluable if you're stretched for time. Just think, you'll be able to pick up a few ingredients, fresh or ready-made, knowing that they'll combine beautifully with all those store-cupboard goodies at home.

Now, just because food is cooked in minutes instead of hours doesn't mean you have to compromise on great taste and presentation — even with classics like Coq au Vin or Cassoulet, or, indeed, my 20-minute Peking Duck. They all look fabulous and taste wonderful. Perhaps you're looking for a complete roast dinner in less than an hour, or stunning snacks in five minutes flat. Yes, there's not a lot you can do in five minutes in the kitchen is there? Feeling smart? How's about breathtaking dazzling desserts like my Zapped Lemon Curd Pudding or my Choco-nana Brandy Snaps, both ready in less than twelve minutes?

7 introduction

8 time-saving ideas

10 getting stocked up

12 equip yourself

14 soups, snacks, salads

42 vegetarian

66 fish

94 poultry

128 meat

162 desserts

190 index

introduction

So . . . why meals in minutes? Well, the amount of times people have come up to me, especially in supermarkets, occasionally in the dry cleaner's, now and then in the florist's and also in the men's room, and asked me to recommend a delicious recipe that can be put together in minutes rather than hours is quite staggering! I discovered that these people all had something in common: some worked strange shifts, some were loaded with children, but generally it was a case of working hard and playing hard, yet everyone wanted to eat fantastic home-cooked food in a flash. So, I wanted to write a book and make a television series that would hopefully give them food for thought and answer all those culinary conundrums. And here it is!

Believe me, once you get into *Meals in Minutes*, your enthusiasm for good, simple nosh becomes more and more infectious. You'll be able to bounce into your kitchen knowing that whatever is hanging around can be quickly whipped into a gourmet feast. Food shopping will be done with confidence – invaluable if you're stretched for time. Just think, you'll be able to pick up a few ingredients, fresh or ready-made, knowing that they'll combine beautifully with all those pantry goodies at home.

Now, just because food is cooked in minutes instead of hours doesn't mean you have to compromise on great taste and presentation – even with classics like my Coq au Vin or Cassoulet, or, indeed, my 20-minute Peking Duck. They all look fabulous and taste wonderful. Perhaps you're looking for a complete roast dinner in less than an hour, or stunning snacks in five minutes flat. Yes, there's not a lot you can do in five minutes in the kitchen, is there? Feeling smart? How's about breathtaking dazzling desserts like my Zapped Lemon Curd Dessert or my Choco-nana Brandy Snaps, both ready in less than twelve minutes? Oooh you lucky people. Go on, get into meals in minutes, discover the art of the perfect pantry, lots of brilliant kitchen tips, and fast, fabulous food.

Enjoy!

time-saving ideas

While most of us aspire to a tasty, varied, and nutritious diet, in most of our hectic lives, time is of the essence when it comes to getting down to business in the kitchen. To help save your energy and get the most out of your time spent at the stove, I've come up with a few handy tips that I always bear in mind when cooking for my own family.

Make your kitchen comfortable

From good lighting to uncluttered work surfaces, in order to get the most out of your cooking you've got to have a pleasant environment in which to work. I always have music on when I'm cooking – yeah, okay – and sometimes a bit of TV, too . . . but if you're enjoying cooking, it will show in the food you create.

Keep it tidy

Do try to keep your kitchen tidy – I always keep equipment I know I'm going to use often, such as my food processor, close to hand and other items such as my electric juicer tucked away ready for when I do need to use them. It also saves you lots of time in the long run if you do the dishes as you go along. Never leave this until after you've eaten the meal; instead try to clear up as much as possible before you go to sit down and save yourself the hassle of dealing with it all later.

Sort out your pantry

Keep your pantry tidy – regularly throw out items that are out of date and arrange things logically. I always put little stickers on the top of my jars of herbs and spices so I can find what I want without having to rifle through every single jar. As we all know, the one you're looking for is normally the last one you find.

Get the right tools for the job

Ensuring that you've got the right equipment saves you a heck of a lot of time. This is a good example: if you want to mash potatoes, then get a good, solid potato masher; don't try doing it with a flimsy, plastic little number or, worse still, a fork! – it takes all day! Better still, invest in an electric beater – they make the best mash ever. And as for knives, buy good ones and keep them sharp; they're much safer to use and get the chopping done a lot more efficiently. See Equip Yourself on pages 12-13 for more information.

Preparing meals ahead

Many of the dishes in this book can be cooked in advance and then simply reheated. Others can be prepared ahead and just need to be cooked when you're ready to eat. Take the time to plan what you're going to cook and prepare as much as you can as far ahead as possible – you'll save yourself time and worries later.

Making the most of convenience foods

Convenience foods are out there to make our lives easier – make the most of them (see pages 10-11 for more information).

Make double and freeze half

It's well worth making double quantities of suitable dishes, then freezing half – it doesn't take all that much longer and you know that you've got a tasty, nutritious meal ready if you just haven't got time to cook.

Use the services on offer

Ask your butcher to dice your meat or bone out your leg of lamb for you and get your fish counter to fillet, skin, and bone your fish – they're there to help you, so make good use of their skills and save yourself a lot of time.

getting stocked up

One of the best-kept secrets of the clever cook's success is a well-stocked larder. From basic essentials such as milk and eggs to the latest in convenience foods such as Mexican flour tortillas – if you keep yourself as well stocked as I am, you'll never run short of ideas when it comes to putting together a tasty meal in minutes. Of course, there are lots of items in my pantry, some of which just may not be your regular staples, so either avoid them or swap them for similar items you prefer – after all, cookery is all about experimentation.

Pantry essentials

Canned foods

chopped plum tomatoes
corn
baked beans
chickpeas
red kidney beans
coconut milk
tuna
anchovies
black olives
pimientos (sweet red peppers)
custard
sliced fruit in natural juice

Bottles and jars

sunflower oil, for everyday frying
extra virgin olive oil, for
    salad dressings
sesame oil, for stir-fries and
    Oriental-style dishes
white wine vinegar and
    balsamic vinegar
soy sauce
wholegrain and Dijon mustard
tomato ketchup
Worcestershire sauce
Tabasco or other chile sauce
curry paste
pesto sauce
sun-dried tomato paste
black olive paste (tapenade)
mayonnaise
crunchy peanut butter
Marmite (yeast extract)
clear honey
jam
vanilla extract
wine: red and white
sherry or port
brandy

Dried goods

English mustard powder
baking powder
baking soda
small package all-purpose flour
small package self-rising flour
cornstarch
spaghetti
pasta shapes such as penne or rigatoni
egg noodles
rice: long-grain, basmati and risotto
couscous
sugar: superfine, light raw brown,
    confectioners'
bouillon cubes
herbs and spices: oregano, black
    peppercorns, ground cumin, paprika,
    cayenne, dried chile flakes, curry powder
    or paste
dried fruit: raisins/golden raisins,
apricots/prunes
nuts: slivered almonds, unsalted peanuts
bread/pizza dough mix

In the refrigerator

milk
eggs
unsalted butter
spreadable butter
whipping cream, crème fraîche or Greek
yogurt
soft cheese or Mascarpone
Parmesan
sharp Cheddar
bacon

In the freezer

As well as buying ready-frozen items, I like to freeze a lot of my own stuff, too.

ginger root: peel 1 inch (2.5 cm) pieces of ginger root, cover in freezer film, and freeze – it's much easier to grate when frozen and means you'll always have a supply handy

herbs: any left-over fresh herbs can be packed in strong plastic bags and stored in the freezer – they're really good for cooking with and when you need to use them, just pull off a handful and crumble them into your pan – no need to chop!

bread: most bread freezes very well

garden peas
leaf spinach
vanilla ice cream
ready-rolled puff pastry

Groceries

green onions
tomatoes
garlic
onions
potatoes
oranges and lemons
bread: take your pick from the incredible
    range now available – I like to use soft
    flour tortillas, standard sliced bread, and
    longer-life part-baked breads,
    such as Italian ciabatta

equip
yourself

Make life easier for yourself by getting
well equipped – you don't need a lot of
gear, but it makes sense if you buy the
best that you can afford: then you know
it'll work for you and last longer than a
cheaper counterpart. It is also very
important if you are opting for cheaper
equipment to ensure that it is safe –
avoid any flimsy equipment and make
sure that saucepans and knives have
strong handles.

Here's a list of basic equipment that
you would do well to stock up on – and
don't forget, each piece you buy should
be treated as an investment, as many
high-quality items have very long
guarantees.

The basics

1 large sharp knife
1 small sharp knife
1 chef's steel/knife
 sharpener
can opener
2 chopping boards
large frying pan
3 sizes of saucepan
 with lids
3 wooden spoons
set of kitchen scales
colander
measuring jug
metal hand whisk
metal sieve
slotted spoon
fish slice

potato masher
swivel-style vegetable
 peeler
box-style cheese
 grater
pastry brush
rolling pin
roasting pan
baking sheet
casserole dish with lid

Handy extras

As well as the essentials,
here's a list of items that
will often prove pretty handy
in the kitchen.

lemon zester
tongs
potato ricer
palette knife
hand-held blender
food processor
garlic press
wok
rubber spatula
lemon juicer
tea strainer
flour dredger

soups, snacks, salads

17	CHICKEN AND CORN SOUP	20 MINS
18	CLAM CHOWDER WITH PARMESAN CROUTONS	30 MINS
19	SNAPPY ZAPPED STUFFED TATTIES	25 MINS
20	CLARE'S CHILE BEAN RANCH PASTIES	35 MINS
22	CARAMELIZED TUNA TATTIES	25 MINS
23	CRISPY BATTON BACON POTATO CAKES	35 MINS
24	AINSLEY'S EGGPLANT SUPPER STACKS	25 MINS
27	CHEESY CHERRY TOM POTATO OMELET	25 MINS
28	SUNNY-SIDE HASH 'N' HAM	30 MINS
29	MELTING EGGY-BREAD SANDWICH	20 MINS
30	FLASHED SMOKED SALMON BAGELS	10 MINS
33	SPIKED GREEN ONION SUPPER CRÊPES	25 MINS
34	FINGER-LICKING CHICKEN WINGS	40 MINS
36	TEASING TURKEY PITA POCKETS	20 MINS
38	HONEYED TARRAGON QUICK CHICK SALAD	20 MINS
41	PEPPY'S POSH POTATO SALAD	30 MINS

chicken and corn soup

A popular soup traditionally from the southwest of China. It's deliciously easy to make and thoroughly heart-warming. You can also try making it with a can of creamed corn – if so, leave out the cornstarch, as it's already quite thick.

SERVES 2 | **PREPARATION: 5 MINS | COOKING TIME: 15 MINS**

1 tablespoon vegetable oil
1 x 4 oz (100 g) skinless, boneless chicken breast, finely diced
1 garlic clove, finely chopped
a ½ inch (1 cm) piece ginger root, finely chopped
1 tablespoon cornstarch
2½ cups hot chicken stock
½ cup corn kernels
1 egg
1 tablespoon fresh lemon juice
shredded green onions, to garnish
dark soy sauce and shrimp chips, to serve
toasted sesame seeds to garnish

Heat the oil in a deep pan and gently cook the chicken, garlic, and ginger for 3–4 minutes without coloring.

Blend the cornstarch with a little stock and add to the soup pan with the remaining stock and the corn. Bring to a boil, stirring continuously, and simmer gently for 5–7 minutes.

Beat together the egg and lemon juice and slowly trickle into the soup pan, stirring with a chopstick or fork to make egg strands. Season to taste, garnish with green onions and toasted sesame seeds, and serve with a drizzle of soy sauce and some shrimp chips.

NUTRITION NOTES PER SERVING: calories 271 | protein 17 g | carbohydrate 23.6 g fat 12.8 g | saturated fat 2.26 g | fiber 0.8 g | added sugar 3.37 g | salt 1.52 g

clam chowder with parmesan croutons

Clam chowder is often thought of as a luxurious dish, but this is very easy to make and uses canned clams, which are widely available from supermarkets.

SERVES 4 | PREPARATION: 15 MINS | COOKING TIME: 15 MINS

2 tablespoons butter

4 slices smoked bacon,
  cut into ½ in (1 cm) wide strips

1 onion, finely chopped

1 teaspoon chopped fresh rosemary
  or ¼ teaspoon dried rosemary

8 oz (225 g) floury potatoes, diced

1¼ cups milk

⅔ cup heavy cream

4 oz (100 g) cod fillet, diced

1 x 10½ oz (290 g) can clams in brine

salt and pepper

2 tablespoons chopped
  fresh parsley

FOR THE CROUTONS

2 thick slices country-style bread

2 tablespoons
  freshly grated Parmesan

1 crushed garlic clove

2 tablespoons olive oil

Heat the butter in a small pan and gently cook the bacon, onion, and rosemary for 6–7 minutes until softened and golden.

Meanwhile, place the potatoes in a pan with the milk and cream and cook gently for 10–15 minutes until tender.

Preheat the oven to 425°F (220°C). To make the croutons, cut the bread into large dice and toss with the Parmesan, garlic, olive oil, and plenty of seasoning. Scatter onto a baking sheet and roast in the oven for 5–8 minutes, turning occasionally until crisp and golden brown.

Using a potato masher, gently crush the potatoes into the cream mixture, but take care not to over-mash; there should still be several chunks of potato in the soup. Stir in the bacon mixture, the cod, and the clams, including the liquid in the can. Simmer very gently for 3–4 minutes until the cod is cooked.

Season to taste and stir in the chopped parsley. Ladle into bowls and scatter over the Parmesan croutons.

NUTRITION NOTES PER SERVING: calories 589 | protein 23.3 g | carbohydrate 31.8 g fat 41.8 g | saturated fat 21.21 g | fiber 1.5 g | added sugar none | salt 3.24 g

snappy zapped stuffed tatties

If you want crispy potato skins, pop them under a hot broiler briefly after you've microwaved them, then cut a cross in the top of each, squeeze them up carefully, add the sensationally easy-to-make topping, and enjoy.

SERVES 4 | **PREPARATION: 10 MINS | COOKING TIME: 15 MINS**

4 x 9 oz (250 g) baking potatoes, unpeeled
8 slices smoked bacon, roughly chopped
2 leeks, cut into thin strips
6 green onions, sliced
4 oz (100 g) full-fat soft cheese
salt and pepper
4 tablespoons sour cream and cayenne pepper, to serve

Scrub, dry and prick the potatoes with a fork. Arrange well apart on a double thickness of paper towels. Cook in a microwave on high for 6 minutes; then turn and cook for another 6–7 minutes until tender. Leave to stand for 2 minutes. If you don't have a microwave, cook for 1 hour at 425°F (220°C) in a preheated oven – longer if you want crispy skins.

Meanwhile, cook the bacon in a nonstick frying pan for 3–4 minutes until crisp. Add the leeks and green onions and stir-fry for a few minutes until wilted. Add the soft cheese and stir until it melts. Remove from the heat and season to taste with salt and pepper.

Cut a cross in the top of each potato, gently squeeze the bottom to open out, and pile the filling into the center. Serve topped with a dollop of sour cream and a sprinkling of cayenne pepper.

NUTRITION NOTES PER SERVING: calories 506 | protein 13 g | carbohydrate 45 g fat 31 g | saturated fat 16 g | fiber 4 g | added sugar none | salt 2.03 g

clare's chile bean ranch pasties

These really are packed full of flavor and the kids just love 'em – so does the wife, Clare, too.

SERVES 4 | PREPARATION: 15 MINS | COOKING TIME: 20 MINS

1 tablespoon sunflower oil
4 slices smoked bacon, cut into strips
1 small onion, finely chopped
1 garlic clove, finely chopped
1 x 7 oz (200 g) can baked beans
2 oz (50 g) sharp Cheddar, finely diced
a few drops of Tabasco sauce
13 oz (375 g) package ready-rolled puff pastry
milk, for brushing
mixed leaf salad, to serve

Preheat the oven to 425°F (220°C). Heat the oil in a small pan and cook the bacon, onion, and garlic for 4–5 minutes until golden. Remove from the heat and mix with the baked beans and diced cheese; add Tabasco to taste.

Open out the pastry and cut into quarters to make four 8 x 4½ inch (20 x 11 cm) rectangles. Spoon the filling into the center of each; then bring up the edges to enclose the filling. Press the edges together to create a seam across the center of each pasty. Transfer to a baking sheet, brush with a little milk, and bake for 12–15 minutes until puffed and golden brown.

Serve with salad and watch them disappear.

NUTRITION NOTES PER SERVING: calories 580 | protein 15.1 g | carbohydrate 44.1 g
fat 39.4 g | saturated fat 7.09 g | fiber 2.2 g | added sugar 1.7 g | salt 2.58 g

caramelized tuna tatties

Dress up baked potatoes with mini mountains of rich golden onions, tuna, feta cheese, and grilled cherry tomatoes. Just the description gets my juices flowing.

SERVES 2 | PREPARATION: 5 MINS | COOKING TIME: 20 MINS

2 x 9 oz (250 g) baking potatoes, unpeeled
10 cherry tomatoes
1 tablespoon butter
1 tablespoon olive oil
1 large onion, thinly sliced
1 x 3¼ oz (85 g) can tuna in brine, drained
4½ oz (120 g) feta cheese, cubed
salt and pepper

Scrub and dry the potatoes, then prick several times with a fork. Place well apart on a double thickness of paper towels; then microwave on high for 6 minutes. Turn and cook for another 6–7 minutes until tender. Allow to stand for 2 minutes. If you don't have a microwave, cook for 1 hour at 425°F (220°C) in a preheated oven – longer if you want crispy skins.

Preheat the broiler to high. Place the potatoes and tomatoes on a baking sheet and broil for 4–5 minutes until the potato skins crisp up and the tomatoes just begin to split; keep warm.

Meanwhile, melt the butter with the oil in a small pan and cook the onion for 10 minutes, stirring occasionally until softened and golden. Stir in the tuna and cook for 2–3 minutes to warm through; season to taste.

Cut a deep cross in the top of each potato and squeeze the bottom gently to open them up. Fill with the tuna mixture, then top with the grilled tomatoes and feta; season to taste and serve immediately.

NUTRITION NOTES PER SERVING: calories 426 | protein 22.2 g | carbohydrate 42.9 g fat 19.7 g | saturated fat 11.92 g | fiber 4.7 g | added sugar none | salt 2.97 g

crispy batton bacon potato cakes

These soft, fluffy potato cakes are great any time of day or night but I love to eat them topped with a fried egg – owright, and a can of baked beans – for the perfect lazy breakfast.

SERVES 4 | **PREPARATION: 10 MINS | COOKING TIME: 25 MINS**

1 lb 2 oz (500 g) floury potatoes, diced
1 tablespoon olive oil
4 slices smoked bacon, cut into ¾ in (2 cm) wide strips
½ cup grated sharp Cheddar
1 teaspoon English mustard
4 green onions, finely chopped
½ cup all-purpose flour
a knob of butter
salt and pepper

Cook the potatoes in boiling, salted water for 10–15 minutes until tender.

Heat the oil in a large frying pan and cook the bacon strips for 3–4 minutes until crisp and well browned.

Drain the potatoes and mash well; stir in the crispy bacon, Cheddar, mustard, green onions, flour, and plenty of salt and pepper. Shape the mixture into eight even-size cakes.

Heat the butter in the bacon pan and gently cook the potato cakes for 3–4 minutes on each side until well browned.

NUTRITION NOTES PER SERVING: calories 318 | protein 10.2 g | carbohydrate 31.6 g
fat 17.5 g | saturated fat 7.6 g | fiber 2.1 g | added sugar none | salt 1.39 g

ainsley's eggplant supper stacks

A great crunchy veggie supper that looks good, tastes good and, by golly, probably does you good.

SERVES 4	**PREPARATION: 10 MINS	COOKING TIME: 15 MINS**

4 x ½ inch (1 cm) thick eggplant slices, cut on the diagonal
1 tablespoon all-purpose flour
1 egg, beaten
8 tablespoons fresh white breadcrumbs
2 tablespoons freshly grated Parmesan
1 teaspoon dried thyme
3 tablespoons olive oil, plus extra for drizzling
1 garlic clove, sliced
2 tomatoes, sliced
4 large slices French or Italian bread, cut on the diagonal
4 oz (100 g) Mozzarella, sliced
salt and pepper
mixed salad leaves, to serve

Coat the eggplant slices in the flour; then dip in the egg. Mix together the breadcrumbs, Parmesan, and thyme, and use to coat the slices.

Heat the olive oil in a frying pan and cook the garlic for 30 seconds; then remove and discard. Fry the eggplant in the same pan for 5–8 minutes, turning once, until tender and golden; remove and keep warm. Cook the tomatoes briefly in the same pan, then remove and keep warm.

Preheat the broiler to high. Toast the bread on both sides; then drizzle one side with any pan oil or extra olive oil. Lay the cheese on the bread and broil until it starts to melt. On the serving plates arrange the fried tomato slices over the cheese and top with eggplant. Serve with the mixed salad leaves.

NUTRITION NOTES PER SERVING: calories 454 | protein 18.8 g | carbohydrate 57.2 g fat 18.4 g | saturated fat 6.06 g | fiber 2.6 g | added sugar none | salt 2.1 g

cheesy cherry tom potato omelet

Eggs must be one of the most convenient foods. They're the ideal friendly fast food that requires hardly any cooking time, so . . . roll up, roll up for this eggy fiesta feast.

SERVES 2   PREPARATION: 10 MINS | COOKING TIME: 15 MINS

½ cup grated Edam or Mozzarella
4 cherry tomatoes, quartered
4 small cooked new potatoes, sliced
1 tablespoon snipped fresh chives
4 eggs
a knob of butter
½ teaspoon olive oil
salt and pepper

Mix together the grated cheese, tomato quarters, potato slices, and snipped chives. Beat together the eggs and a little seasoning in a separate bowl.

Melt the butter and oil in a 9–10 inch (23–25 cm) frying pan; then pour in the beaten egg. As the omelet cooks, use a fork to gather the set egg into the center of the pan so the runny egg can run to the edge to cook. Continue to cook over a low heat for several minutes until just set.

Preheat the broiler to high. Tilt the pan; then use a spatula to roll up the omelet. Carefully transfer to a warm, heatproof plate ensuring that the join is underneath.

Cut a slit along the top and spoon in the tomato and chive mixture. Place under the broiler for 1 minute to melt the cheese and warm the filling. Season with salt and pepper and serve hot.

NUTRITION NOTES PER SERVING: calories 301 | protein 20 g | carbohydrate 11 g fat 20 g | saturated fat 8 g | fiber 1 g | added sugar none | salt 1.58 g

Spice up this dish by sprinkling over a little Worcestershire or Tabasco sauce.

sunny-side hash 'n' ham

This simple, classic dish, topped with fried eggs, will keep your sunny side up.

SERVES 2 | PREPARATION: 10 MINS | COOKING TIME: 20 MINS

1 lb (450 g) floury potatoes, diced
2 tablespoons olive oil
1 x 6 oz (175 g) ham steak, diced
8 oz (225 g) savoy cabbage, thinly sliced
scant ½ cup vegetable stock
1 tablespoon chopped fresh parsley
2 eggs
salt and pepper

Cook the potatoes in a pan of boiling, salted water for 5–7 minutes until just tender; drain well.

Heat 1 tablespoon of the olive oil in a frying pan and cook the ham and potatoes for 5 minutes, stirring occasionally, until the potatoes are crisp and golden; remove the ham and potatoes from the pan and set aside. Stir the cabbage and stock into the same pan and cook for 6–8 minutes until tender; season to taste and stir in the parsley. Return the ham and potatoes to the pan and keep warm.

Meanwhile, heat the remaining oil in a small nonstick frying pan; crack in the eggs and cook for 3–4 minutes until set.

Divide the potato mixture between two serving plates and top each with a fried egg; season to taste and serve immediately.

NUTRITION NOTES PER SERVING: calories 562 | protein 28.4 g | carbohydrate 39.1 g fat 33.5 g | saturated fat 9.36 g | fiber 6.3 g | added sugar 0.5 g | salt 3.26 g

melting eggy-bread sandwich

You didn't think eggy bread could get any better, did you? Well, a bit of oozy cheese and some tasty ham make my eggy-bread sandwich just about the most satisfying snack you could ask for.

SERVES 1 | PREPARATION: 10 MINS | COOKING TIME: 10 MINS

¼ cup grated Gruyère or Mozzarella
1 cherry tomato, roughly diced
1 slice of cooked ham, cut into thin strips
2 fresh basil leaves, roughly torn, or a pinch of dried oregano
2 slices of white bread
1 egg
2 tablespoons milk
1–2 tablespoons olive oil or 2 tablespoons butter
salt and pepper

Mix together the cheese, tomato, ham, and basil or oregano; season to taste. Sprinkle the mixture over one slice of bread and place the other slice on top, pressing down firmly to make a sandwich.

Beat the egg, milk, and a little seasoning together in a shallow dish; lay the sandwich in the mixture and leave to soak for 2–3 minutes. Turn the sandwich over and leave for another 2–3 minutes until all the liquid has been absorbed.

Heat the olive oil or butter in a large frying pan and gently cook the sandwich for 3–4 minutes on each side until puffed and golden. Drain on paper towels and serve immediately.

NUTRITION NOTES PER SERVING: calories 487 | protein 24.5 g | carbohydrate 36.1 g
fat 28.2 g | saturated fat 9.48 g | fiber 1.2 g | added sugar none | salt 2.71 g

Don't be tempted to cook the sandwich over too high a heat as it will brown very quickly, before the cheese inside has melted.

flashed smoked salmon bagels

Smoked salmon comes ready to eat but I find that a quick flash in the pan changes the texture and offers a deliciously different way to enjoy it. Perhaps it's the creamy, soft egg, runny yolk, and charred salmon . . . what do you think?

SERVES 2   PREPARATION: 5 MINS | COOKING TIME: 5 MINS

2 eggs
1 bagel
a small knob of butter
2 slices smoked salmon
2 tablespoons crème fraîche
1 tablespoon snipped fresh chives
salt and pepper

Preheat the broiler to high. Boil the eggs in a small pan for 4 minutes. Meanwhile, halve the bagel and place under the hot broiler for 1–2 minutes until toasted. Spread with a little butter.

Heat a small nonstick frying pan and then cook the smoked salmon slices for 30 seconds on one side only.

Place the toasted bagel halves on two serving plates and ruffle the cooked smoked salmon on top. Spoon over a dollop of crème fraîche. Drain and shell the eggs and place one on top of the crème fraîche. Season to taste, sprinkle with chives, and serve immediately.

NUTRITION NOTES PER SERVING: calories 338 | protein 24.8 g | carbohydrate 22.7 g fat 17.1 g | saturated fat 7.48 g | fiber 0.7 g | added sugar none | salt 3.74 g

SOUPS | SNACKS | SALADS

spiked green onion supper crêpes

You might find your own favorite filling with enough practice, but this little lot really does the trick. Pancake-packed with crêpe flavors – yes please!

SERVES 4 | **PREPARATION: 10 MINS | COOKING TIME: 15 MINS**

9 oz (250 g) new potatoes, sliced
4 oz (100 g) green beans, sliced
6 slices bacon, chopped
1 small onion, chopped
sour cream and chile powder,
   to serve
watercress, to garnish

FOR THE CRÊPES
1 cup all-purpose flour
a pinch of salt
2 eggs
1¼ cups milk
1 tablespoon vegetable oil,
   plus extra for frying
4 green onions, finely chopped
2 tablespoons chopped fresh parsley

To make the crêpes beat together the flour, salt, and eggs. Gradually beat in the milk to make a smooth batter; then stir in 1 tablespoon of the oil, the green onions, and parsley.

Steam the potatoes over a pan of boiling water for 3 minutes; add the beans and continue to cook for another 7 minutes until both are tender.

Heat a little vegetable oil in an 8–9 inch (20–23 cm) nonstick frying pan; then pour in enough batter to coat the bottom evenly. Cook for about 2 minutes until golden underneath; then turn and cook for 1 minute. Keep the crêpes warm while you repeat three times with the remaining batter.

Heat a little oil in a frying pan and cook the bacon and onion for 4–5 minutes until golden; add the potatoes and beans, and gently warm through.

Fold the crêpes into triangles to make pockets and fill with the bacon mixture. Top each with a spoonful of sour cream and a sprinkling of chile. Garnish with the watercress and serve.

NUTRITION NOTES PER SERVING: calories 426 | protein 16 g | carbohydrate 39 g
fat 24 g | saturated fat 9 g | fiber 3 g | added sugar none | salt 1.9 g

finger-licking chicken wings

Chicken wings are inexpensive, cook quickly, and make fabulous finger food. Try eating these without licking your fingers!

SERVES 4	PREPARATION: 5 MINS | COOKING TIME: 35 MINS

1 tablespoon vegetable oil
1 small onion, very finely chopped
2 garlic cloves, crushed
2 tablespoons clear honey
4 tablespoons tomato ketchup
4 tablespoons Worcestershire sauce
2 teaspoons English mustard
2 teaspoons Tabasco sauce
8 chicken wings, tips removed
2 tablespoons flour, seasoned with salt and pepper

Preheat the oven to 400°F (200°C).

Heat the oil in a small pan and cook the onion and garlic for 3–4 minutes until softened. Stir in the honey, ketchup, Worcestershire sauce, mustard, and Tabasco, and simmer very gently for a minute or so.

Dust the chicken in the seasoned flour; then brush liberally with the sauce. Place on a baking sheet and roast for 30 minutes until well browned and cooked through.

Transfer to a serving plate and keep those napkins handy, or just lick those fingers!

NUTRITION NOTES PER SERVING: calories 440 | protein 24.3 g | carbohydrate 33.1 g fat 24.4 g | saturated fat 5.69 g | fiber 1.6 g | added sugar 13 g | salt 1.54 g

teasing turkey pita pockets

You can't beat a good tease when hungry, so for a casual lunchtime or afternoon snack you can't go far wrong with my turkey pita pockets. They'll tease your tastebuds right 'til the last bite.

SERVES 4	PREPARATION: 10 MINS | COOKING TIME: 10 MINS

1 tablespoon vegetable oil
a knob of butter
1 onion, thinly sliced
2 garlic cloves, finely chopped
1 cup fresh white breadcrumbs
6 fresh sage leaves, finely chopped
grated rind and juice of 1 lemon
½–1 teaspoon Cajun seasoning or mild chile powder
7 oz (200 g) cooked turkey, cut into ½ inch (1 cm) strips
salt and pepper
4 pita breads
shredded iceberg or romaine lettuce, sliced red onion, and 4 tablespoons
   sour cream or Greek yogurt, to serve
wedges of lemon (optional)

Heat the oil and butter in a large frying pan and cook the onion and garlic for 3–4 minutes until softened and golden. Stir in the breadcrumbs, sage, lemon rind, Cajun seasoning, and turkey, and stir fry for 2–3 minutes until the breadcrumbs begin to brown. Add the lemon juice and season to taste.

Make a slit in the side of each pita. Mix together the lettuce and red onion and pack into the bottom of each pita pocket. Pile in the turkey mixture and top with a dollop of sour cream or Greek yogurt and, if you like, a squeeze of lemon juice.

NUTRITION NOTES PER SERVING: calories 414 | protein 23.9 g | carbohydrate 62 g
fat 9.5 g | saturated fat 3.01 g | fiber 2.7 g | added sugar none | salt 1.73 g

We like a
bit of that,
don't we?
Yes we do!

honeyed tarragon quick chick salad

I like to cook the chicken on a griddle pan, which gives the chicken lovely markings and a smoky taste, but a frying pan or wok does the job just as well. A bottle or two of iced lager beer goes down a treat.

SERVES 2 | PREPARATION: 15 MINS | COOKING TIME: 5 MINS

3 tablespoons olive oil
grated rind and juice of 1 lemon
1 garlic clove, chopped
1 tablespoon chopped fresh tarragon
2 x 4 oz (100 g) boneless, skinless chicken breasts, each cut into 6–7 slices
1 teaspoon sesame oil
1–2 teaspoons clear honey
1 tablespoon toasted sesame seeds
3 slices Italian-style bread such as foccacia or ciabatta, toasted and halved
salt and pepper
lettuce leaves and watercress, to serve and garnish

In a small bowl, mix together 2 tablespoons of the olive oil, the lemon rind, 1 teaspoon of lemon juice, the garlic, tarragon, and salt and pepper. Rub the mixture over the chicken slices; then cook in a heated griddle, nonstick frying pan, or wok, for 4–5 minutes until golden brown.

Meanwhile, make the dressing: mix together the remaining olive oil and lemon juice with the sesame oil, honey, and sesame seeds; season with salt and pepper.

Place three pieces of toast on each serving plate and scatter over the lettuce and watercress. Arrange the chicken slices on top; then spoon over the dressing. Garnish with watercress and serve.

NUTRITION NOTES PER SERVING: calories 634 | protein 39 g | carbohydrate 42 g fat 35 g | saturated fat 6 g | fiber 2 g | added sugar 4 g | salt 1.9 g

SOUPS | SNACKS | SALADS

peppy's posh potato salad

A simple, snazzy salad that makes a posh sunshine supper for two, and is bound to be a contender for this year's summer favorite. It's delicious served with some crusty garlic bread. "But, hey, why wait for the summer?" as my late mother Peppy would have said.

SERVES 2 | PREPARATION: 10 MINS | COOKING TIME 20 MINS

9 oz (250 g) small new potatoes
3 oz (75 g) green beans
4 green onions, diagonally sliced
¾ cup pitted black olives
2 oz (50 g) thinly sliced salami, cut into quarters

FOR THE DRESSING
3 tablespoons olive oil
1 tablespoon white wine vinegar
1 tablespoon chopped fresh mint
2 teaspoons grainy mustard
salt and pepper

Cook the potatoes in a pan of boiling salted water for **15 minutes**; then add the beans and cook for another **3 minutes** until tender but still crisp. Cool under running cold water; then drain and leave to cool.

Cut the potatoes into chunks and toss gently in a serving bowl with the beans, green onions, olives, and salami.

Make the dressing: mix together the oil, vinegar, mint, and mustard; season to taste. Pour over the potato salad and lightly toss together. Divide between two serving plates and serve.

NUTRITION NOTES PER SERVING: calories 388 | protein 9 g | carbohydrate 23 g fat 30 g | saturated fat 7 g | fiber 4 g | added sugar trace | salt 3.36 g

vegetarian

45	CHEESE 'N' ONION TARTE TATIN	50 MINS
46	SPINACH AND BLUE CHEESE TART	50 MINS
49	MEDLEY OF MUSHROOM RISOTTO	35 MINS
50	SILVANA'S PAN-FRIED PIZZA ITALIANA	40 MINS
52	BUBBLING WEBBED-CHEESE PASTA	25 MINS
53	CORTA SPINI-CHILE PASTA	30 MINS
55	YUM YUM NUTTY NOODLES	20 MINS
56	TINGLING THAI-SPICED VEGETABLES	30 MINS
59	SPICY BEANBURGERS	25 MINS
60	SPECKLED-EYE SQUASH STEW	45 MINS
61	SPAGHETTI MOUNT PESTO	30 MINS
62	MIGHTY MEXICAN TORTILLA CHEESECAKE	35 MINS
64	"ARRIBA" SPEEDY GONZALES TORTILLAS	25 MINS
65	GUADIANA TORTILLA OLÉ	45 MINS

cheese 'n' onion tarte tatin

We've done it with apples, we've done it with pears, now do it with onions and watch it disappear. Nothing ever tasted this good upside down.

SERVES 4 | **PREPARATION: 15 MINS | COOKING TIME: 35 MINS**

2 tablespoons butter
1 tablespoon olive oil
3 large red onions, thinly sliced
2 tablespoons dark raw brown sugar
1 tablespoon balsamic vinegar
1¼ cups grated Cheddar
4 oz (115 g) plain pastry, thawed if frozen
mixed salad, to serve

Preheat the oven to 400°F (200°C). Melt the butter with the oil in a large frying pan and cook the onions, stirring occasionally, for 5–8 minutes until softened. Stir in the sugar and vinegar, and cook for another 2 minutes until the sugar dissolves. Spoon into an 8 inch (20 cm) ovenproof pie dish or layer cake pan.

Reserve ¼ cup of the cheese and sprinkle the rest over the onions. Roll the pastry out to a round slightly larger than the dish; then press it lightly over the cheese, tucking down the sides. Prick gently with a fork and bake for about 25 minutes until the pastry is golden and the filling bubbles up around the edge.

Set aside for a few minutes; then place a serving plate on top and invert. While still warm, sprinkle over the reserved cheese, cut into wedges, and serve with the salad.

NUTRITION NOTES PER SERVING: calories 388 | protein 10 g | carbohydrate 28 g
fat 27 g | saturated fat 14 g | fiber 2 g | added sugar 8 g | salt 0.78 g

spinach and blue cheese tart

When you fancy a quick nibble, there's nothing like a slice of blue cheese tart – hot or cold. It's simply delicious.

SERVES 4	PREPARATION: 10 MINS | COOKING TIME: 40 MINS

¼ cup butter
1 small onion, finely chopped
1 garlic clove, finely chopped
12 oz (350 g) fresh spinach
5 x 12 inch (30 cm) square sheets phyllo pastry
3 oz (75 g) Stilton
3 eggs
5 tablespoons crème fraîche
¼ teaspoon ground nutmeg, plus extra for sprinkling
salt and pepper
fresh mixed salad and new potatoes, to serve

Preheat the oven to 350°F (180°C).

Lightly grease an 8 x 1½ inch (20 x 4 cm) loose-bottomed quiche pan. Melt half the butter in a pan and cook the onion and garlic for 5 minutes until softened. Stir in the spinach and cook for a few minutes until wilted. Turn the mixture into a sieve and press well with a wooden spoon to squeeze out any excess liquid.

Melt the remaining butter. Lay one sheet of phyllo across the bottom of the pan with the edges slightly overhanging the sides. Brush well with melted butter. Repeat with the remaining sheets, arranging them at different, overlapping angles.

Spoon the spinach into the bottom of the pastry shell; then crumble over the Stilton. Beat together the eggs, crème fraîche, nutmeg, and salt and pepper. Pour into the pastry shell and sprinkle over a little more nutmeg. Bake for 30 minutes until the filling is set and the pastry golden. Cool a little; then carefully remove from the oven and transfer to a baking sheet. Return to the oven for 5 minutes to crisp up the edges of the tart. Serve with salad and new potatoes.

NUTRITION NOTES PER SERVING: calories 396 | protein 14 g | carbohydrate 18.4 g fat 30 g | saturated fat 16.82 g | fiber 2.2 g | added sugar 0.6 g | salt 1.97 g

medley of mushroom risotto

I love Italian food, and there's not much that can beat a creamy mushroom risotto, especially one served with juicy, garlicky greens. Oh yes, let those juices flow!

SERVES 2 | PREPARATION: 5 MINS | COOKING TIME: 30 MINS

½ oz (15 g) dried cep or
  porcini mushrooms
1¼ cups boiling water
2½ cups vegetable stock
2 tablespoons olive oil
1 small onion, finely chopped
2 garlic cloves, finely chopped
1¼ cups risotto rice
¼ cup butter
9 oz (250 g) mixed fresh mushrooms
  such as flat field, chestnut,
  button, porcini

4 tablespoons chopped fresh
  flat-leaf parsley
2 tablespoons freshly grated
  Parmesan, plus extra to serve
salt and pepper

FOR THE GARLICKY GREENS
2 tablespoons olive oil
2 garlic cloves, finely chopped
9 oz (250 g) fresh spinach or
  4 oz (100 g) shredded
  spring greens
salt

Place the dried mushrooms in a bowl and pour over the boiling water. Keep the stock ready in a pan on a low heat, and have a ladle handy. Heat 1 tablespoon of olive oil in a large saucepan and cook the onion and garlic for 3–4 minutes until softened. Add the rice and cook for 1 minute more. Keeping the heat fairly high, add a ladle full of hot stock to the rice and stir until it has been absorbed. Continue to ladle in the stock gradually, stirring until it has all been absorbed. Remove the soaked mushrooms from the liquid and add to the risotto. Gradually stir in the soaking liquid and continue to cook until the rice is almost tender and the liquid has been absorbed.

Meanwhile, heat the remaining oil and a knob of the butter in a frying pan and cook the mushrooms over a high heat for 3–4 minutes. Stir the fried mushrooms, parsley, Parmesan, and remaining butter into the risotto pan and season to taste; remove from the heat and cover to keep warm. To prepare the greens, heat the oil in a wok or deep frying pan and cook the garlic for 1 minute. Throw in the greens and stir-fry for 1–2 minutes until wilted. Season with salt. Spoon the risotto into serving bowls and pile the wilted greens in the center. Shave Parmesan on top of the greens and serve. Buon appetito!

NUTRITION NOTES PER SERVING: calories 871 | protein 22 g | carbohydrate 103.1 g fat 44 g | saturated fat 18.27 g | fiber 5.9 g | added sugar none | salt 3.04 g

VEGETARIAN

49

silvana's pan-fried pizza italiana

If you think making pizza takes loads of time and effort kneading and tossing, then have a go at my little beauty . . . Mamma mia! You're in for a treat!

SERVES 2   PREPARATION: 15 MINS | COOKING TIME: 25 MINS

FOR THE TOMATO SAUCE

1 tablespoon olive oil
2 garlic cloves, finely chopped
2 green onions, finely chopped
1 x 7 oz (200 g) can
   chopped tomatoes
a handful of fresh basil, roughly torn
1 tablespoon tomato ketchup
salt and pepper
mixed leaf salad, to serve

FOR THE TOPPINGS

1 tablespoon olive oil,
   plus extra for drizzling
4 oz (100 g) button mushrooms,
   thinly sliced

1 garlic clove, finely chopped
1 tablespoon chopped
   fresh parsley
salt and pepper
1 plum tomato, sliced
2 oz (50 g) Mozzarella, sliced
1 teaspoon capers or 1 tablespoon
   pitted black olives

FOR THE DOUGH

2 cups self-rising flour
pinch of salt
2 tablespoons freshly
   grated Parmesan
⅔ cup warm water
2 tablespoons olive oil

To make the tomato sauce, heat the oil in a small pan and cook the garlic and green onions for 2–3 minutes until softened. Stir in the tomatoes, basil, tomato ketchup, and a little seasoning. Bring to a boil and simmer for 5–10 minutes until thickened. To prepare the mushrooms, heat the oil in a small frying pan and cook the mushrooms and garlic for 3–4 minutes until softened. Stir in the parsley and season. Preheat the broiler to medium.

To make the dough, sift the flour and salt into a large bowl; stir in the cheese. Make a well in the center and stir in the water and 1 tablespoon of oil to make a soft dough; then roll into a 10 inch (25 cm) round. Heat the remaining oil in a skillet or ovenproof frying pan and cook the dough for 5–6 minutes until the underside is golden brown. While the dough is cooking, spoon over the tomato sauce and scatter over the toppings. Drizzle over a little oil and place the skillet under a medium broiler for 3–4 minutes until the top is golden and the bottom is cooked through. Cut into wedges and serve with lots of leafy salad.

NUTRITION NOTES PER SERVING: calories 739 | protein 22.7 g | carbohydrate 93.2 g
fat 33.2 g | saturated fat 8.51 g | fiber 6 g | added sugar 1 g | salt 2.74 g

bubbling webbed- cheese pasta

We all know how incredibly versatile pasta is, but what you add to it makes all the difference. So . . . for a wonderful, moreish pasta indulge yourself with my webbed cheesy nosh. If you don't have Mozzarella, use Cheddar or Gruyère instead.

SERVES 2 | **PREPARATION: 10 MINS | COOKING TIME: 15 MINS**

3 tablespoons olive oil

1 orange bell pepper, cut lengthwise into thin strips

1 yellow bell pepper, cut lengthwise into thin strips

½ teaspoon superfine sugar

9 oz (250 g) rigatoni or penne

2 garlic cloves, finely chopped

1 small onion, finely chopped

1 lb 2 oz (500 g) tub puréed tomatoes

3 oz (75 g) soft cheese

a handful of fresh basil leaves

5 oz (150 g) Mozzarella, roughly cut into ½ inch (1 cm) cubes

salt and pepper

mixed salad, to serve

Heat 2 tablespoons of olive oil in a large frying pan and add the bell pepper strips and superfine sugar. Cook over a fairly high heat for 10 minutes, stirring regularly until the peppers are very soft and golden brown. Meanwhile, cook the pasta in a large pan of boiling, salted water according to package directions, until tender. Drain well and return to the pan. Heat the remaining olive oil in a small pan and cook the garlic and onion for 2–3 minutes until softened. Stir in the puréed tomatoes and the soft cheese, stirring until the cheese melts and the sauce turns pink. Turn the heat to the lowest setting and simmer the sauce very gently. Add salt and pepper to taste.

Stir together the pasta, caramelized peppers, and tomato sauce. Roughly tear the basil leaves and stir them into the mixture; then transfer to a heatproof serving dish. Push the cubes of Mozzarella into the pasta, leaving most of them near the surface, and grind plenty of black pepper over the top. Place under a preheated broiler for 3–4 minutes until the cheese is melted and bubbling. Spoon onto serving plates and serve with a crisp, green salad.

NUTRITION NOTES PER SERVING: calories 1059 | protein 42.5 g | carbohydrate 123.9 g fat 47.2 g | saturated fat 12.85 g | fiber 8.6 g | added sugar 8.8 g | salt 3.05 g

corta spini-chile pasta

If you like it hot, hot, hot, like I sometimes do, use a full teaspoon of chile –
if you prefer a milder flavor, simply halve that amount. Tube pasta like
caserecce or rigatoni is best, as the little pockets get filled with the
succulent sauce of stringy cheese.

SERVES 4   PREPARATION: 10 MINS | COOKING TIME: 20 MINS

1 small eggplant, cut lengthwise into ½ inch (1 cm) slices
2–3 tablespoons olive oil
1 onion, chopped
2 garlic cloves, chopped
1 x 14 oz (400 g) can chopped tomatoes
1 teaspoon dried chile flakes
12 oz (350 g) pasta shapes, such as rigatoni or caserecce
4 oz (100 g) frozen leaf spinach
1 cup grated Cheddar or Gruyère
salt and pepper

Preheat the broiler to hot. Lightly brush the eggplant with oil and broil for
2–3 minutes on each side until golden brown. Meanwhile, heat 1 tablespoon of
the oil in a pan and cook the onion and garlic for 3–4 minutes until golden. Stir
in the tomatoes and chile flakes. Bring to a boil and simmer for 4–5 minutes. Cut
the broiled eggplant slices into strips, add to the tomato sauce, and cook for
another 4–5 minutes; season to taste.

Cook the pasta according to the package directions, adding the spinach for the
last 3 minutes. Drain well and return to the pan; then stir in the tomato sauce
and half the cheese. Transfer to serving plates and scatter over the remaining
cheese.

NUTRITION NOTES PER SERVING: calories 416 | protein 16.8 g | carbohydrate 54.9 g
fat 16 g | saturated fat 6.48 g | fiber 4.8 g | added sugar none | salt 0.83 g

*You can use 7 oz (200 g) fresh spinach when it's in season: when the
pasta is cooked, remove from the heat and stir in the trimmed
spinach; then drain.*

yum yum nutty noodles

If you like it hot, nutty and speedy, you simply can't go wrong with this dish. Remember what they say: there's nothing like a good toss of the wok on a weekday night.

SERVES 2 | PREPARATION: 10 MINS | COOKING TIME: 10 MINS

1 x 3½ oz (85 g) package vegetable-flavored instant noodles
2 teaspoons clear honey
1 tablespoon dark soy sauce
1 tablespoon olive oil
a 1 in (2.5 cm) piece fresh ginger root, grated
2 garlic cloves, thinly sliced
2 carrots, sliced
½ red bell pepper and ½ yellow bell pepper, seeded and sliced
6 oz (175 g) very small broccoli florets
4 oz (100 g) chestnut mushrooms, thinly sliced
6 green onions, shredded
½ cup salted cashew nuts

Cook the noodles according to the package directions, then drain. Blend the honey, soy sauce, and 1 tablespoon of water in a bowl and set aside.

Heat the oil in a large frying pan or wok. Add the ginger, garlic, carrots, bell peppers, broccoli, and mushrooms, and stir-fry over a high heat for 3–4 minutes until crisp but tender. Add the green onions and stir-fry for 1 minute more. Toss the noodles with the vegetables and sauce and heat through; then spoon onto plates. Serve sprinkled with the cashews.

NUTRITION NOTES PER SERVING: calories 511 | protein 17.8 g | carbohydrate 63.1 g fat 22.5 g | saturated fat 0.9 g | fiber 8.3 g | added sugar 11.5 g | salt 1.36 g

To give the carrots a decorative look, cut in half lengthwise, cut two thin v-shaped grooves lengthwise down each half, then cut into diagonal slices.

tingling thai-spiced vegetables

Get those tastebuds tingling with this trendy Thai delight. Simply toss those veggies in a pan and stir in the heavenly sauce. I've served them on a bed of couscous, but you could use rice or pasta.

SERVES 4   **PREPARATION: 10 MINS | COOKING TIME: 20 MINS**

2 tablespoons vegetable oil

1 onion, sliced

1 lb 7 oz (650 g) mixed vegetables, such as carrots, broccoli, celery,
    green beans, and eggplants, chopped

2–3 teaspoons Thai red curry paste

1¼ cups vegetable stock

1¾ cups couscous

1½ cups boiling water or vegetable stock

scant 1 cup coconut cream

salt and pepper

½ cup chopped peanuts, to garnish

Heat the oil in a large pan and cook the sliced onion for 3–4 minutes until golden. If using carrots, add them before the other vegetables and fry for 2 minutes; then add the remaining vegetables and cook for another 3 minutes. Stir in the curry paste and stock, cover and simmer for 10 minutes until the vegetables are tender but still firm.

Place the couscous in a bowl and pour over the boiling water or stock. Let stand for 4–5 minutes, fluffing up with a fork two or three times until the couscous becomes light and crumbly.

Stir the coconut cream into the vegetables, heat through and season. Divide the couscous between four plates, top with spicy vegetables, and scatter over the chopped peanuts.

NUTRITION NOTES PER SERVING: calories 516 | protein 13 g | carbohydrate 45 g
fat 33 g | saturated fat 17 g | fiber 7 g | added sugar none | salt 0.99 g

spicy
beanburgers

My beanburgers are nutritious, easy to make and taste great. The kids love to prepare them, and can't wait to eat them. If it's a nice day, why not slap 'em on the barbie?

SERVES 2 | PREPARATION: 15 MINS | COOKING TIME: 10 MINS

1 tablespoon vegetable oil
1 small onion, finely chopped
2 garlic cloves, finely chopped
1 small, hot, red chile, finely chopped
4 oz (100 g) frozen chopped spinach, thawed
1 x 14 oz (400 g) can cannellini beans
1 cup fresh white breadcrumbs
1 teaspoon ground cumin
1 tablespoon chopped fresh cilantro
salt and pepper
burger buns, relish, and salad, to serve

Heat the oil in a small saucepan and cook the onion, garlic, and chile for 5 minutes until softened. Squeeze the excess moisture out of the spinach and place in a large bowl.

Mash the beans well and mix with the spinach, breadcrumbs, cumin, and cilantro. Add the fried onion mixture and stir well together.

Season to taste and shape into four round burgers. Broil or shallow fry for a few minutes on each side until crisp and golden. Serve in burger buns with relish and salad.

NUTRITION NOTES PER SERVING: calories 302 | protein 14.5 g | carbohydrate 47 g fat 7.5 g | saturated fat 0.73 g | fiber 10.4 g | added sugar none | salt 0.94 g

speckled-eye squash stew

This stew positively oozes goodness, yet is easy to make and tastes terrific. But the real beauty is that it's all made in one delicious pot.

SERVES 3 | PREPARATION: 15 MINS | COOKING TIME: 30 MINS

2 tablespoons olive oil
½ teaspoon cumin seeds
½ teaspoon mustard seeds
1 onion, chopped
1 garlic clove, finely chopped
1 red chile, seeded and sliced
1 lb (450 g) potatoes, roughly chopped
2 tablespoons curry paste
2½ cups vegetable stock
1 lb (450 g) squash (butternut, pumpkin, or kabocha), roughly diced
1 x 14 oz (400 g) can black-eyed peas, drained
2 tomatoes, each cut into six wedges
salt and pepper
2 tablespoons chopped fresh cilantro or parsley, to garnish
warm naan bread and lemon wedges, to serve

Heat the olive oil in a large pan, add the seeds, and cook for 1 minute; when they begin to splutter and pop, add the onion, garlic, and chile and cook for 3–4 minutes until softened. Stir in the potatoes and cook for 3 minutes. Add the curry paste and vegetable stock. Bring to a boil and simmer for 5 minutes. Add the squash and simmer for another 15 minutes until the vegetables are tender. Add the black-eyed peas and tomatoes, and continue to cook for 2–3 minutes; season to taste.

Divide the stew between serving plates or large shallow bowls and sprinkle over the cilantro or parsley. Serve with naan bread and lemon wedges.

NUTRITION NOTES PER SERVING: calories 377 | protein 14.2 g | carbohydrate 58.1 g fat 11.4 g | saturated fat 1.3 g | fiber 10.5 g | added sugar none | salt 1.37 g

spaghetti
mount pesto

If you're lucky enough to have half a jar of sun-dried tomatoes in the refrigerator, toss them into the spaghetti as well to achieve a really authentic Italian flavor. To get a lovely spiral effect with the spaghetti, twirl it around a long-pronged fork; then slide it onto the plate, creating a mini mountain. Ooh, your guests will be so impressed!

SERVES 4 | **PREPARATION: 10 MINS | COOKING TIME: 20 MINS**

12 oz (350 g) spaghetti
2 tablespoons olive oil, plus extra to serve
1 large yellow bell pepper, seeded and thinly sliced
1 garlic clove, sliced
1 red chile, seeded and sliced
¾ cup peas, thawed if frozen
6 oz (175 g) chestnut mushrooms, sliced
9 oz (250 g) cherry tomatoes, halved
3 tablespoons red pesto sauce
salt and pepper
2 oz (50 g) Parmesan, shaved or grated, to serve

Cook the spaghetti in a pan of boiling salted water according to the package directions. Meanwhile, heat the olive oil in a frying pan, and cook the bell pepper for 2 minutes. Add the garlic, chile, peas, and mushrooms, and stir-fry for another 2–3 minutes until the vegetables are tender but still firm. Remove from the heat and stir in the cherry tomato halves.

Drain the spaghetti, then return to the pan. Stir in the pesto sauce and vegetables and season to taste.

To serve, spoon onto four serving plates, or twirl the pasta around a long-pronged fork and place in mounds on the plates. Scatter with Parmesan shavings, drizzle over a little oil, and serve immediately.

NUTRITION NOTES PER SERVING: calories 512 | protein 21.7 g | carbohydrate 66.2 g
fat 19.8 g | saturated fat 5.22 g | fiber 11.2 g | added sugar none | salt 1.3 g

mighty mexican tortilla cheesecake

Well, not cheesecake as you know it, but delightful layers of flour tortillas filled with saucy beans, vegetables, and grated cheese. Go on . . . get in on the Mexican feast. A few bottles of Mexican lager help it slip down nicely.

SERVES 3   PREPARATION: 10 MINS | COOKING TIME: 25 MINS

1 tablespoon olive oil
1 onion, chopped
½-1 teaspoon hot chile powder
1 x 14 oz (400 g) can chopped tomatoes with herbs
7 oz (200 g) frozen mixed vegetables
1 x 7½ oz (215 g) can kidney beans, drained
5 x 10 inch (25 cm) flour tortillas
1¼ cups grated sharp Cheddar
salt and pepper
shredded lettuce, sour cream, and chopped green onions, to serve

---

Preheat the oven to 350°F (180°C).

Heat the oil in a pan and cook the onion for 3–4 minutes until golden. Stir in the chile powder and tomatoes and cook for 5 minutes, or until slightly thickened. Add the mixed vegetables and heat through for 4 minutes, or until the sauce has thickened. Stir in the beans and heat through; then season.

Place a tortilla on a heatproof plate, spread with a little of the sauce, and sprinkle over a handful of cheese. Continue layering the tortillas, sauce, and cheese, finishing with a sprinkling of cheese. Place the plate on a baking sheet and warm through in the hot oven for 10 minutes until the cheese has melted. Cut into wedges and serve with shredded lettuce, sour cream, and green onions.

NUTRITION NOTES PER SERVING: calories 549 | protein 25.6 g | carbohydrate 65.1 g
fat 22.6 g | saturated fat 11.66 g | fiber 6.3 g | added sugar none | salt 2.42 g

"arriba" speedy gonzales tortillas

Introduce some Mexican magic into your house by serving a stack of these tasty tortillas. If you're making a fresh guacamole, leave the avocado pit in the guacamole to prevent it from going brown - another great tip brought to you by Ainsley!

SERVES 2   PREPARATION: 15 MINS | COOKING TIME: 5-10 MINS

1 tablespoon vegetable oil
1 onion, chopped
1 garlic clove, chopped
1 teaspoon ground cumin
1 x 14 oz (400 g) can kidney beans, drained
3 flour tortillas
½ cup ready-made guacamole
2 tomatoes, seeded and diced
4 crisp lettuce leaves, shredded
½ cup grated Red Leicester
salt and pepper
cilantro sprigs, to garnish (optional)

Heat the oil in a pan and cook the onion for 3-4 minutes until golden. Stir in the garlic and cumin, and cook for 1 minute more. Remove from the heat and stir in the beans. Using a potato masher, roughly crush the mixture; season to taste.

Gently heat the tortillas in a microwave or dry frying pan to make them soft and easy to roll.

Spoon the guacamole over the tortillas and scatter over the lettuce and tomatoes. Spoon the beans on top and scatter over the grated cheese. Roll up each tortilla and slice in half diagonally. Stack three halves on each serving plate and garnish with any remaining lettuce and tomato and cilantro sprigs, if using.

NUTRITION NOTES PER SERVING: calories 605 | protein 23 g | carbohydrate 74 g fat 26 g | saturated fat 7 g | fiber 14 g | added sugar none | salt 2.72 g

VEGETARIAN

guadiana tortilla olé

Tortillas taste great straight from the pan and even when cold. Leftovers are fabulous in a French-bread sandwich with a dollop of mayonnaise or tomato ketchup. And for those who like to add a touch of trivia to mealtimes, the Guadiana is a river in Spain.

SERVES 2 | PREPARATION: 15 MINS | COOKING TIME: 30 MINS

1 lb (450 g) new potatoes, scrubbed
2 tablespoons olive oil
1 large onion, sliced
1 large red bell pepper, seeded and sliced
1 garlic clove, crushed
4 eggs, beaten
2 tablespoons milk
1 tablespoon chopped fresh parsley or 1 teaspoon dried parsley
salt and pepper

Cook the potatoes in boiling water for **10–15 minutes** until just tender. Drain and slice.

Meanwhile, heat the oil in a small, deep frying pan and gently cook the onion and bell pepper for about **5 minutes** until softened and the onion is beginning to turn golden. Add the sliced potatoes and the garlic, and cook for another **5 minutes**, stirring occasionally.

Beat together the eggs, milk, parsley, and seasoning, and pour over the vegetables. Turn the heat to the lowest setting and cook gently for about **8 minutes** until the mixture is almost completely set – keep checking the underside to make sure it doesn't burn.

Use a fish slice to turn the tortilla over carefully or, if it's a little tricky, place a plate over the pan, invert the tortilla onto the plate, and then slide it back into the pan. Cook for another **2–3 minutes** until the underside is golden brown. Cut into wedges and serve. Olé!

NUTRITION NOTES PER SERVING: calories 488 | protein 19.5 g | carbohydrate 52.5 g fat 23.7 g | saturated fat 4.99 g | fiber 5.6 g | added sugar none | salt 0.71 g

VEGETARIAN

fish

69	ADMIRED AVOCADO SALSA PASTA	30 MINS
70	GOLDEN TUNA FISH TRIANGLES	30 MINS
71	WICKED WILD FISH GUMBO	40 MINS
72	FAB HADDIE AND GOOEY EGG	25 MINS
74	SAUCY SALMON AND LEEK PAN PIZZA	30 MINS
75	WAN KAI THAI-STYLE RED CURRY	20 MINS
77	WICKED WINE-STEAMED MUSSELS	20 MINS
78	TOSSED BEANSPROUT SHRIMP NOODLE	15 MINS
81	SIMPLY SMOKIN' PAELLA	35 MINS
82	COD KEBABS WITH AZTEC SALSA	30 MINS
85	CRUNCH LUNCH COD AND MASH	30 MINS
86	CHILE-LEMON-SPLASHED FISH	30 MINS
88	CITRUS-CRUSTED COD WITH CAJUN SPUDS	30 MINS
89	ROCKY ROAD POTATO COD	60 MINS
90	GARLIC BUTTER SOLE WITH CITRUS MASH	25 MINS
92	CAWLEY'S CLASSIC FISH AND CHIPS	30 MINS

admired avocado salsa pasta

Talk about a feast for the eyes. This warm pasta salad is so full of color, texture, and life it will win gasps of admiration even before the first bite.

SERVES 4 | **PREPARATION: 15 MINS | COOKING TIME: 15 MINS**

12 oz (350 g) pasta bows or spirals
½ small red onion, finely chopped
1 avocado, skinned, pitted, and finely diced
4 tomatoes, seeded and finely diced
2 tablespoons chopped fresh cilantro
2 tablespoons fresh lime juice
3 tablespoons olive oil
2 garlic cloves, chopped
1 red chile, seeded and thinly sliced
6 oz (175 g) fresh or canned crabmeat
salt and pepper
ground cayenne pepper, to garnish

Cook the pasta in plenty of boiling salted water according to the package directions. Meanwhile, make the avocado salsa: mix together the red onion, avocado, tomatoes, cilantro, lime juice, and 1 tablespoon of the olive oil. Season the salsa with salt and pepper and set aside.

Heat the remaining oil in a small pan and cook the garlic and chile for 30 seconds. Add the crabmeat to the pan and heat through briefly.

Drain the pasta and return to the pan; then stir in the warmed crabmeat mixture. Stir in half of the avocado salsa and divide between four warmed serving plates. Spoon over the remaining avocado salsa and sprinkle with a little ground cayenne pepper to garnish.

NUTRITION NOTES PER SERVING: calories 537 | protein 19 g | carbohydrate 71 g
fat 22 g | saturated fat 3 g | fiber 6 g | added sugar none | salt 0.6 g

golden tuna fish triangles

Tuna from the pantry often comes to our rescue when we want a quick ingredient, and once you've tasted these, you'll agree that this is one of the best ideas yet. Spice it up with a seeded, chopped green chile.

SERVES 4   PREPARATION: 10 MINS | COOKING TIME: 20 MINS

1 lb (450 g) potatoes, peeled and cubed
1 x 7 oz (200 g) can tuna in brine, drained
4 green onions, finely chopped
2 tablespoons chopped fresh cilantro or parsley
4 tablespoons sour cream
grated rind of 1 lime or ½ lemon
2 tablespoons vegetable oil
1 tablespoon all-purpose flour
paprika, for dusting
salt and pepper
leafy green salad, cooked corn cobs, cut into thick slices,
   and sweet chile sauce, to serve

Cook the potatoes in boiling water for **10–12 minutes**. Drain and mash well; then stir in the tuna, green onions, cilantro or parsley, sour cream, and lime rind. Season to taste. Divide into eight portions and shape into triangles.

Heat the oil in a nonstick frying pan. Dust the fish triangles with flour and cook for 3 minutes on each side until golden; drain on paper towels and dust lightly with paprika. Serve with salad, corn cob slices, and a spoonful of sweet chile sauce.

NUTRITION NOTES PER SERVING: calories 230 | protein 11.6 g | carbohydrate 24.6 g fat 10.1 g | saturated fat 3.24 g | fiber 1.7 g | added sugar none | salt 0.56 g

To make a quick sweet chile sauce, mix 4 tablespoons tomato ketchup, 1 tablespoon clear honey, ¼ teaspoon chile powder, and the juice of ½ lemon.

wicked wild fish gumbo

Gumbo is synonymous with southern American cuisine, and, just like a classic stew, everything is cooked in one pot – a real fireside meal. Although you can't be perched on a rock overlooking the Mississippi river, it's equally delicious in front of your log fire or radiator. You can use any combination of fish, but avoid oily ones like herring and mackerel.

SERVES 4   **PREPARATION: 15 MINS | COOKING TIME: 25 MINS**

2 tablespoons olive oil
1 onion, chopped
2 garlic cloves, thinly sliced
1 red chile, seeded
 and thinly sliced
1 fennel bulb, sliced
1 lb (450 g) floury potatoes, diced
2 fresh rosemary sprigs or
 ½ teaspoon dried rosemary
⅔ cup dry white wine
1 x 14 oz (400 g) can chopped
 tomatoes

1–2 tablespoons sun-dried tomato
 paste or regular tomato paste
1½ pints fish stock
1 lb 7 oz (650 g) mixed fish fillets,
 such as cod, haddock, and salmon,
 skinned and cut into chunks
2 tablespoons chopped fresh dill
4 tablespoons sour cream
salt and pepper
warm French bread or croutons,
 to serve

Heat the olive oil in a large pan and cook the onion for 1 minute. Add the garlic, chile, fennel, and potatoes, and stir-fry for another 3–4 minutes. Add the rosemary and wine, bring to a boil, and cook rapidly for 2 minutes. Stir in the tomatoes, paste, and stock and return to a boil; then simmer for 10 minutes until thickened slightly.

Add the fish and simmer gently for 4 minutes until just cooked; season to taste. Ladle into serving bowls and sprinkle with the dill; drizzle over the sour cream and serve with French bread or large, crunchy croutons.

NUTRITION NOTES PER SERVING: calories 413 | protein 34.4 g | carbohydrate 27.7 g fat 16.4 g | saturated fat 4.47 g | fiber 3.8 g | added sugar none | salt 1.47 g

This dish is delicious served with croutons. To make them, heat 3–4 tablespoons of olive oil in a frying pan. Tear half a small French stick into pieces and stir-fry until crisp and golden. Drain on paper towels.

fab haddie and gooey egg

This is the best double-act in town, and makes a super light and easy evening meal. The swirling water helps to pull the egg white together to form a well-shaped poached egg. Serve it with chunks of your favorite flavored bread, such as olive ciabatta. Encourage your guests to break the yolk when it gets to the table – ooh, just watch it flow.

SERVES 4 | PREPARATION: 10 MINS | COOKING TIME: 15 MINS

1 tablespoon olive oil
1 onion, sliced
1 x 14 oz (400 g) can chopped tomatoes
2 tablespoons chopped fresh parsley, plus extra to garnish
4 x 4 oz (100 g) pieces smoked haddock, skinned
2 tablespoons white wine vinegar
4 eggs
salt and pepper
steamed broccoli, to serve

Heat the oil in a large frying pan and cook the onion for 4–5 minutes until golden. Stir in the tomatoes and parsley, and season with salt and pepper. Place the fish pieces on top, cover and simmer for about 8 minutes until the fish is cooked.

Meanwhile, add the vinegar to a medium pan of boiling water; then lower the heat slightly and swirl the water around with a spoon. Crack two of the eggs into two separate cups; then gently slide both eggs into the swirling water. Cook for 2–3 minutes until the white is set but the yolk is still runny. Remove and drain with a slotted spoon; keep warm. Repeat with the other two eggs.

Spoon the sauce and fish onto serving plates. Top each with an egg, sprinkle with parsley, and season with pepper. Serve with the broccoli.

NUTRITION NOTES PER SERVING: calories 218 | protein 29 g | carbohydrate 6 g
fat 9 g | saturated fat 2 g| fiber 1 g | added sugar none | salt 3.95 g

saucy salmon and leek pan pizza

Another brilliant idea that's ready in a flash. I always like a piquant sauce or topping to go with my salmon, and this little lot is a scrumptious treat. So . . . what's on TV tonight?

SERVES 4 | **PREPARATION: 15 MINS | COOKING TIME: 15 MINS**

1½ cups all-purpose flour, plus
extra for dusting
2 teaspoons baking powder
1 tablespoon olive oil,
plus extra for brushing
salt and pepper

FOR THE TOPPING
1 tablespoon olive oil
2 leeks, sliced

scant 1 cup crème fraîche
2 tomatoes, roughly chopped
1 x 7½ oz (215 g) can salmon,
drained and flaked
1 cup grated Mozzarella or
Cheddar
2 tablespoons black olives
salt and pepper
small fresh dill sprigs, to serve

Mix together the flour, baking powder, and a little salt and pepper. Make a well in the center and mix in 1 tablespoon olive and a scant ½ cup cold water to make a soft dough; knead lightly on a floured surface until smooth.

Roll the dough out to make an 11 inch (28 cm) round. Brush a 12 inch (36 cm) frying pan with a little oil and place over a moderate heat. Add the dough and cook for 3–4 minutes. Turn and cook the other side for another 4–5 minutes until cooked through.

Meanwhile, make the topping: heat the olive oil in a separate frying pan and cook the leeks for 4–5 minutes until softened. Preheat the broiler to high. Spread 5 tablespoons of the crème fraîche onto the pizza base; then scatter over the leeks, tomatoes, salmon flakes, cheese, and olives. Season with salt and pepper. Broil the pizza for 2–3 minutes until the cheese is golden; then spoon small dollops of crème fraîche over the top. Sprinkle with the dill sprigs and serve.

NUTRITION NOTES PER SERVING: calories 573 | protein 21.9 g | carbohydrate 40.2 g fat 37.1 g | saturated fat 17.92 g | fiber 3.2 g | added sugar none | salt 2.36 g

wan kai thai-style red curry

Thai-style curries are very "in" at the moment. We all seem to love the combination of exotic spices with that creamy coconut taste. And to think you can have all this in about 15 minutes – it's well worth trying. The curry paste I use is available in most large supermarkets.

SERVES 4 | PREPARATION: 5 MINS | COOKING TIME: 15 MINS

1 tablespoon sunflower oil
1 onion, thinly sliced
2 tomatoes, roughly diced
1 x 14 oz (400 g) can coconut milk
1 tablespoon Thai red curry paste
1 lb 2 oz (500 g) cubed, skinned white fish such as cod, haddock or coley
juice of ½ lemon
1 tablespoon soy sauce
a handful of fresh basil or cilantro leaves
salt and pepper
cooked rice and steamed sugar-snap peas or snow peas, to serve

Heat the sunflower oil in a large, nonstick pan and cook the onion over a high heat for 4–5 minutes until beginning to brown. Add the tomatoes and cook for 1 minute; then stir in the coconut milk and curry paste. Bring to a gentle simmer and add the fish; cook gently for 4–5 minutes until the fish is just tender.

Stir in the lemon juice, soy sauce, and fresh herbs, and season to taste. Spoon the rice into serving bowls and gently ladle over the fish curry; serve with sugar snap peas or snow peas.

NUTRITION NOTES PER SERVING: calories 172 | protein 23.3 g | carbohydrate 9.3 g fat 4.9 g | saturated fat 0.62 g | fiber 1.7 g | added sugar none | salt 1.47 g

wicked wine-steamed mussels

I love mussels! They're cheap, quick and easy to cook yet still really sophisticated – and cooked like this they're sure to slip down a treat!

SERVES 2 | **PREPARATION: 10 MINS | COOKING TIME: 10 MINS**

⅔ cup dry white wine
1 small onion, very finely chopped
2 garlic cloves, thinly sliced
1 red chile, seeded and finely chopped, or a pinch of dried chile flakes
2¼ lb (1 kg) scrubbed live mussels
a handful of fresh parsley, roughly chopped
black pepper
French bread and green salad, to serve

Pour the wine into a large saucepan with a close-fitting lid. Add the onion, garlic, and chile and bring to a boil. Simmer for 5 minutes until the onion is tender.

Meanwhile, check the mussels, discarding any that remain open when tapped sharply with a knife (if they don't close, they're dead and should not be eaten). Add the mussels to the pan with a good grinding of black pepper. Cover and steam for 3–5 minutes, shaking the pan occasionally, until all the shells have just opened. Discard any that do not open after cooking.

Sprinkle the parsley over and ladle the mussels and the wine juices into large bowls. Serve with plenty of bread and salad.

NUTRITION NOTES PER SERVING: calories 178 | protein 19.8 g | carbohydrate 5.5 g
fat 3.3 g | saturated fat 0.55 g | fiber 1.7 g | added sugar none | salt 1.13 g

Mussels, which you can buy from fall through to spring, are naturally quite salty, so don't go mad on the seasoning.

tossed beansprout shrimp noodle

When we buy shrimp they are often frozen. You can get small pink ones up to large tiger shrimp, which can be a lot more expensive, but are truly worth it for that special occasion. So, if you're feeling a bit flash, use tiger shrimp, but if you're feeling unoysterish, use another type of mushroom.

SERVES 2 | **PREPARATION: 10 MINS | COOKING TIME: 5 MINS**

6 oz (175 g) medium egg noodles
2 tablespoons vegetable oil
1 garlic clove, chopped, or 1 teaspoon garlic purée
1 tablespoon chopped fresh cilantro or parsley
6 green onions, diagonally sliced
1 red chile, seeded and chopped
4 oz (100 g) mushrooms, such as oyster, chestnut, or button, sliced
4 oz (100 g) large cooked, peeled shrimp
3 tablespoons oyster sauce
1 tablespoon fresh lime juice
2 teaspoons superfine sugar
4 oz (100 g) fresh beansprouts
fresh cilantro or parsley sprigs, to garnish

Cook the noodles for 4 minutes, or according to the package directions, then drain well.

Meanwhile, heat the vegetable oil in a frying pan and stir-fry the garlic, cilantro or parsley, green onion slices, and chile for 1 minute. Add the mushrooms and shrimp, and stir-fry for 1 minute longer.

Stir in ½ cup water, the oyster sauce, lime juice, and sugar; cook briefly to heat through and reduce slightly. Stir in the noodles and beansprouts, and heat through. Garnish with a sprinkling of cilantro or parsley, toss and serve. May I recommend chop sticks?

NUTRITION NOTES PER SERVING: calories 560 | protein 29 g | carbohydrate 70 g
fat 20 g | saturated fat 2 g | fiber 2 g | added sugar trace | salt 5.32 g

simply
smokin' paella

And no, I don't mean put it in a pipe or set it alight. I'm talking about smoked ham, which gives this easy-peasy paella a distinctive flavor. Another dish that's cooked in one pot – that'll save on the washing up.

SERVES 4 | PREPARATION: 10 MINS | COOKING TIME: 25 MINS

2 tablespoons vegetable oil
1 onion, sliced
1 red bell pepper, seeded and diced
1 garlic clove, crushed
generous 1 cup long-grain rice
6 oz (175 g) smoked ham, roughly diced
3¾ cups chicken or vegetable stock
½ teaspoon each paprika and turmeric
6 oz (175 g) large shrimp, thawed if frozen
⅔ cup frozen peas
salt and pepper

Heat the oil in a large frying pan and cook the onion for 3–4 minutes until softened and golden. Add the red bell pepper, garlic, and rice, and stir-fry for 1 minute. Add the ham, stock, paprika, and turmeric; bring to a boil and simmer for 12 minutes.

Stir in the shrimp and peas, and cook for another 3–4 minutes until the rice and vegetables are tender. Season to taste; then divide between four serving plates and serve immediately. Ooh, how about a glass of Rioja?

NUTRITION NOTES PER SERVING: calories 380 | protein 25 g | carbohydrate 52 g fat 10 g | saturated fat 2 g | fiber 3 g | added sugar none | salt 4.12 g

Saffron is the traditional method for giving paella its yellow color, but it is expensive. If you do have some, replace the turmeric and paprika with a large pinch of saffron threads.

cod kebabs with aztec salsa

This dish presents beautifully, and is ideal for a quick meal. My lively lime marinade really firms up the fish nicely for broiling. To add an extra kick to your salsa, simply add one small, fresh, seeded, chopped chile.

SERVES 3   PREPARATION: 15 MINS | COOKING TIME: 15 MINS

1 lb (450 g) skinned thick
   cod fillets, cubed
grated rind of 1 lime
juice of 2 limes
3 tablespoons olive oil
3 tomatoes, seeded and chopped
1 small red onion, finely chopped

1 tablespoon chopped fresh
   parsley or cilantro
1 tablespoon drained capers
1 zucchini, diagonally sliced
8 oz (225 g) tagliatelle
salt and pepper

Mix together the cubed cod, lime rind, half the lime juice, and 1 tablespoon of the oil. Season with salt and pepper and set aside to marinate for 5 minutes.

Mix the tomato flesh, onion, 1 tablespoon of the oil, the parsley or cilantro, capers, and the remaining lime juice.

Preheat the broiler to high. Thread the cod cubes and zucchini slices onto six bamboo skewers; season and broil for 8–10 minutes, turning once, until tender and golden.

Meanwhile, cook the tagliatelle in a large pan of boiling, salted water, according to package directions. Drain, then toss with the remaining oil. Fork some tagliatelle into the center of each plate, top with two kebabs, and spoon over some salsa.

NUTRITION NOTES PER SERVING: calories 504 | protein 37 g | carbohydrate 61 g
fat 14 g | saturated fat 2 g | fiber 4 g | added sugar none | salt 0.74 g

If using wooden or bamboo skewers, first soak them in warm water for 10 minutes to prevent them burning.

crunch lunch
cod and mash

You can buy all manner of smoked fish: trout, eel, mackerel, salmon, cod and kippers (known as herrings before they get kippered), to name but a few. Remember to look for nice moist flesh when buying. This snappy dish is ready to serve in a flash.

SERVES 4 | PREPARATION: 15 MINS | COOKING TIME: 15 MINS

1 tablespoon butter, plus extra for greasing
4 x 5 oz (150 g) smoked cod fillets, skinned
6 green onions
4 tomatoes, sliced
8 black olives, pitted and chopped
2 tablespoons olive oil
3 tablespoons torn fresh basil leaves
½ cup fresh white breadcrumbs
1 lb 9 oz (700 g) potatoes, chopped
4–5 tablespoons milk
salt and pepper

Preheat the oven to 400°F (200°C).

Place the fish in a buttered ovenproof dish and season. Chop the white parts from the onions, slice, and scatter over the cod. Arrange the tomatoes on top of the fish and scatter over the olives. Drizzle over half the oil and sprinkle with half the basil. Toss the breadcrumbs with the remaining basil, season, and scatter over the fish. Drizzle over the remaining oil and bake for 15 minutes until the fish is cooked.

Meanwhile, cook the potatoes in a pan of boiling, salted water for 10–15 minutes. Drain well; then add the milk and mash to a soft consistency. Push the mash to one side of the pan, add the butter, and heat. Finely chop the green parts of the onions, add to the pan, and fry briefly. Stir the onions into the mash; season.

Divide the onion mash between four serving plates and place the cod on top. Spoon around the fish juices and serve.

NUTRITION NOTES PER SERVING: calories 384 | protein 33 g | carbohydrate 39 g
fat 12 g | saturated fat 3 g | fiber 4 g | added sugar none | salt 5.32 g

chile-lemon-splashed fish

It's fluffy, it's puffy, it's pulling in the crowds. I am, of course, referring to couscous. It's a great pantry standby as it's precooked and is ready to serve in just a couple of minutes. Go on, give it a try – it'll give mealtimes a fluffy feel.

SERVES 4 | **PREPARATION: 15 MINS | COOKING TIME: 15 MINS**

1 lemon
4 x 4½ oz (120g) cod or
   haddock fillets, unskinned
3 tablespoons olive oil,
   plus extra for brushing
2 garlic cloves, finely chopped
1 red bell pepper, seeded
   and finely diced
1¼ cups couscous

1¼ cups hot vegetable stock
2 tomatoes, finely diced
4 green onions, finely chopped
2 tablespoons chopped
   fresh cilantro or parsley
¼ teaspoon chile powder
salt and pepper

Preheat the broiler to high.

Cut four slices from the lemon and squeeze the juice from the remainder into a small bowl. Place the fish fillets on the broiler pan, skin-side up, and lay the lemon slices on top; brush with a little olive oil and season with salt and pepper. Broil for 6–8 minutes, without turning, until cooked and golden.

Meanwhile, heat 1 tablespoon of the olive oil in a large pan and cook the garlic and bell pepper for 4–5 minutes until softened. Stir in the couscous, hot stock, tomatoes, green onions, and cilantro or parsley. Season to taste, cover and remove from the heat.

Mix the lemon juice with the remaining 2 tablespoons of oil and the chile powder. Fork up the couscous until fluffy; then spoon onto serving plates, place the fish on top, and drizzle over the chile dressing.

NUTRITION NOTES PER SERVING: calories 302 | protein 25.8 g | carbohydrate 28.2 g fat 10.1 g | saturated fat 1.42 g | fiber 1.2 g | added sugar none | salt 0.77 g

citrus-crusted cod with cajun spuds

An impressive meal that's full of color, texture, and taste. Try with other types of fish like haddock, salmon, pollock, bream, or sea bass.

SERVES 4 | PREPARATION: 10 MINS | COOKING TIME: 20 MINS

4 x 5 oz (150 g) red-skinned potatoes, cooked and cut into six wedges
3 tablespoons olive oil, plus extra for brushing
1 teaspoon Cajun seasoning or paprika
4 x 5 oz (150 g) cod fillets, skinned
2 tablespoons sun-dried tomato paste
¾ cup fresh white breadcrumbs
1 tablespoon chopped fresh parsley
grated rind and juice of 1 lemon
4 tomatoes, seeded and finely chopped
4 green onions, finely chopped
salt and pepper
steamed broccoli, to serve

Preheat the oven to 425°F (220°C). Arrange the potato wedges on a baking sheet, lightly brush with oil, and sprinkle with Cajun seasoning or paprika and a little salt. Roast for 12–15 minutes until golden brown.

Meanwhile, season the cod fillets and spread each with the sun-dried tomato paste. Mix together the breadcrumbs, parsley, lemon rind, a splash of lemon juice, and some seasoning. Press the crumb mixture on top of the paste-covered fish to make a crust.

Heat 1 tablespoon of the olive oil in a nonstick frying pan. Cook the fish, crust-side down, for 2–3 minutes until golden. Place in an ovenproof dish, crust-side up, and bake for 8–10 minutes until cooked.

To make the salsa, mix the tomatoes, green onion and remaining oil and lemon juice in a bowl and season to taste. Serve the fish with the potato wedges, tomato salsa, and steamed broccoli.

NUTRITION NOTES PER SERVING: calories 360 | protein 31.1 g | carbohydrate 36.6 g
fat 10.9 g | saturated fat 1.5 g | fiber 2.9 g | added sugar none | salt 1.07 g

rocky road potato cod

A mid-week meal that's good for the holidays. Make the pie ahead if you like, chill, then cook for slightly longer. Try to use Idaho Desiree potatoes.

SERVES 4 | **PREPARATION: 15 MINS | COOKING TIME: 45 MINS**

2 lb (900 g) potatoes, cubed
1 lb (450 g) cod fillet, skinned
  and cut into large chunks
6 oz (175 g) peeled shrimp
1 tablespoon vegetable oil
1 onion, chopped
6 slices bacon, chopped
5 oz (150 g) button mushrooms

7 oz (200 g) soft cheese
⅔ cup light cream
4 tablespoons chopped
  fresh parsley
grated rind of 1 lemon
salt and pepper
steamed green vegetables such as
  broccoli and snow peas, to serve

Preheat the oven to 375°F (190°C). Cook the potatoes in a large pan of boiling salted water for 8–10 minutes until almost tender.

Meanwhile, arrange the cod evenly in the bottom of a 1½ quart (1.5 liter) pie dish and scatter over the shrimp. Heat the oil in a pan and cook the onion and bacon for 5 minutes. Add the mushrooms and cook for another minute. Spoon over the fish.

Warm the soft cheese in the same pan until melted; then stir in the cream and half the parsley. Season to taste and pour over the fish. Roughly spoon over the potatoes and sprinkle with the lemon rind and remaining parsley. Season with salt and pepper and bake for 20–25 minutes until the fish is cooked. Place under the broiler, preheated to medium, for 5 minutes until the top is nicely browned.

NUTRITION NOTES PER SERVING: calories 720 | protein 44.1 g | carbohydrate 43.4 g fat 42.2 g | saturated fat 10.95 g | fiber 4.3 g | added sugar none | salt 2.62 g

garlic butter sole with citrus mash

Lemon sole is a super fish with a mild flavor. It is best cooked quickly so it doesn't dry out and retains that subtle flavor. Your fish counter will fillet the whole sole for you - all you need to do is ask.

SERVES 2   **PREPARATION: 10 MINS | COOKING TIME: 15 MINS**

1 lb (450 g) floury potatoes, cubed
a knob of butter, at room temperature
1 garlic clove, crushed
2 tablespoons chopped fresh parsley
2 x 4½ oz (120 g) lemon sole fillets, unskinned
⅔ cup heavy cream
grated rind and juice of 1 lemon
salt and black pepper
steamed vegetables such as snow peas and spinach, to serve

Cook the potatoes in a large pan of boiling, salted water for 10–12 minutes until tender.

Preheat the broiler to high. Meanwhile, mix together the butter, garlic, parsley, a little salt, and plenty of black pepper. Cook the sole skin-side up under the broiler for 1–2 minutes. Turn over the fish, dot with the herbed butter, and return to the broiler for another 2–3 minutes until golden and cooked through.

Meanwhile, heat the cream and lemon rind in a small pan. Drain the potatoes and mash well; then beat in the warm, zesty cream until smooth and fluffy. Season well to taste; then spoon onto serving plates. Arrange the sole fillets on top of the mash and drizzle over a little of the fresh lemon juice. Serve with steamed green vegetables.

NUTRITION NOTES PER SERVING: calories 650 | protein 27.7 g | carbohydrate 41.8 g
fat 42.4 g | saturated fat 25.77 g | fiber 3.5 g | added sugar none | salt 0.76 g

Let those juices flow. Ooh... what am I like?

cawley's classic fish and chips

You can't beat fish and chips and the key to their success is a crispy batter. The brilliant batter in this recipe comes courtesy of my mate Richard Cawley who served up a winner on the TV program *Ready Steady Cook*.

SERVES 2   PREPARATION: 10 MINS | COOKING TIME: 20 MINS

2 large floury potatoes
2 x 6 oz (175 g) cod fillets, unskinned
sunflower oil, for deep-frying
tartar sauce and lemon wedges, to serve

FOR THE BATTER
4 tablespoons all-purpose flour, plus extra for dusting
1 teaspoon baking soda
scant ½ cup cold water
juice of 1 lemon
salt and pepper

Scrub the potatoes in clean, cold water and cut into fingers as thick or thin as you like. Wash well, rinsing off excess starch to stop them sticking together, and dry thoroughly with paper towels. Heat the sunflower oil in a deep frying pan until the oil is hot enough for a cube of bread to turn brown in about 1 minute. Cook the chips for 5–7 minutes, or until pale golden. Remove with a slotted spoon and drain on paper towels. Dust the cod in a little flour, shaking off any excess.

Make the batter: place the flour and baking soda in a bowl and whisk in the water to make a smooth batter. Stir in the lemon juice and a pinch of salt. Dip the dusted cod into the batter, shaking off any excess, and deep-fry in the hot oil for 5 minutes until the batter is deep golden and the fish is cooked through. Drain on paper towels and keep warm. Raise the heat slightly and when the oil is hot enough to brown a cube of bread in 30 seconds, return the chips to the pan for 1–2 minutes until crisp. Drain on paper towels and sprinkle with salt. Serve the crispy fish and chips with a good spoonful of tartar sauce and lemon wedges for squeezing over.

NUTRITION NOTES PER SERVING: calories 712 | protein 38.1 g | carbohydrate 64.7 g fat 35.1 g | saturated fat 4.62 g | fiber 3.7 g | added sugar none | salt 1.32 g

It's easy to make your own tartar sauce – just stir together some mayonnaise with a few chopped pickles, capers, onion, and parsley.

a spicy

poultry

spin on

tradition

97	JIMMY'S CHICKEN KIEV	30 MINS
98	MOZZARELLA-OOZING ROSEMARY CHICKEN	30 MINS
99	TURKEY DUMPLINGS WITH SPICY BROTH	25 MINS
100	LIGHTNING COQ AU VIN	40 MINS
102	ZESTY CHICK FRIC	45 MINS
103	LIVER AND BACON WITH TSAR MASH	15 MINS
104	CLEVER COOK'S ROAST CHICKEN DINNER	40 MINS
107	ACAPULCO CHICKEN	40 MINS
108	CHA-CHA-CHA CHIMICHANGAS	30 MINS
110	SOS CHICKEN WITH PILAU RICE	15 MINS
111	GORGEOUS CHICKEN KORMA	40 MINS
113	DOODLE SPINACH 'N' CHICKEN NOODLE	20 MINS
114	GINGER CHICKEN WITH COCONUT RICE	35 MINS
117	FLASH CHICKEN SATAY	25 MINS
118	CHESTER'S CHICKEN CHOW MEIN	15 MINS
121	CHIANG MAI THAI BOLOGNESE	25 MINS
122	PROSCIUTTO TURKEY ROULADES	20 MINS
125	PEKING DUCK	20 MINS
126	SUCCULENT SPICED DUCKLING	40 MINS

the
al

jimmy's chicken kiev

Chicken Kiev is one of those old favorites that everyone loves, especially my kids. My lima bean purée brings it up to date with a bang!

SERVES 2 | **PREPARATION: 15 MINS | COOKING TIME: 15 MINS**

2 x 3 oz (75 g) boneless, skinless
  chicken breasts
3 tablespoons unsalted butter,
  at room temperature
4 tablespoons chopped
  fresh parsley
2 garlic cloves, crushed
1 cup fresh white
  breadcrumbs
1 tablespoon freshly
  grated Parmesan
1 tablespoon all-purpose flour,
  seasoned with salt and pepper
1 egg, beaten
1–2 tablespoons vegetable oil

FOR THE LIMA BEAN PURÉE
1 tablespoon olive oil
1 small onion, finely chopped
1 x 14 oz (400 g) can lima beans,
  drained
3 oz (75 g) sharp Cheddar
  or Gruyère, finely diced
a knob of butter
2 tablespoons chopped
  fresh cilantro (optional)
a few drops of Tabasco
  or other hot chile sauce
salt and pepper
lemon wedges and green salad,
  to serve

Using a small knife, horizontally cut a pocket into each chicken breast. Mix together the butter, parsley, garlic, and plenty of salt and pepper. Spoon the mixture into the pocket of each chicken breast. Stir together the breadcrumbs and Parmesan. Dust the chicken breasts in the seasoned flour, then the beaten egg and, finally, roll in the breadcrumb mixture. Heat the vegetable oil in a large frying pan and cook the chicken for 5–6 minutes on each side until golden brown and cooked through.

To make the lima bean purée, heat the olive oil in a small pan and cook the onion for 5 minutes until softened. Add the beans to the pan and cook gently for 2–3 minutes, stirring occasionally, until warmed through. Add the cheese to the pan with the butter, stirring until melted. Using a hand blender, whizz the mixture until smooth and creamy. Stir in the cilantro, if using, and add salt, pepper, and Tabasco to taste. Spoon the purée onto serving plates and top with the chicken Kiev. Serve with lemon wedges and crisp green salad.

NUTRITION NOTES PER SERVING: calories 863 | protein 45.3 g | carbohydrate 55.8 g fat 52.5 g | saturated fat 25.07 g | fiber 9.5 g | added sugar none | salt 2 g

mozzarella-oozing rosemary chicken

This is based on a Neapolitan dish. Lots of people think that rosemary was made for lamb, but it goes equally well with chicken. In fact, I think this will get you the "ooh!" approval. Use fresh rosemary if you like, increasing the quantity to two teaspoons of the chopped herb.

SERVES 4	PREPARATION: 10 MINS	COOKING TIME: 20 MINS

5 oz (150 g) Mozzarella, drained
1½ teaspoons dried rosemary
¼ teaspoon dried chile flakes
8 boneless chicken thighs
1 tablespoon all-purpose flour
olive oil, for brushing

1lb 9 oz (700 g) potatoes, cubed
2 tablespoons butter
1 leek, cut into ¼ inch (6 mm) rounds
2 tablespoons milk or light cream
salt and pepper

Preheat the broiler to high. Cut the Mozzarella in half widthwise, then cut each half into four wedges. Mix the rosemary and chile flakes with salt and pepper in a bowl; then toss the cheese in it.

Lay the chicken thighs out flat, sprinkle with the flour, and place a cheese wedge in the center of each. Roll the chicken around the cheese and secure with wooden toothpicks, tucking in the ends, if possible. Place in a roasting pan, brush with oil, season and broil for 20 minutes, turning occasionally, until cooked through.

Meanwhile, cook the potatoes in a pan of boiling, salted water for 10–15 minutes until tender; drain well and keep warm. Melt the butter in a frying pan and stir-fry the leek for 3–4 minutes until softened. Mash the potatoes with the milk or cream; then stir in the leeks and season to taste. Divide the leek mash between four serving plates and remove the toothpicks before placing the chicken on top; spoon round the chicken-pan juices and serve.

NUTRITION NOTES PER SERVING: calories 605 | protein 35 g | carbohydrate 36 g
fat 36 g | saturated fat 15 g | fiber 3 g | added sugar none | salt 1.21 g

turkey dumplings with spicy broth

Okay, it is a bit unusual to see an English-style meatball made with these Oriental flavorings, but trust me, it's fabulous! I have even been known to crumble a few shrimp chips on top just before serving.

SERVES 2 | **PREPARATION: 10 MINS | COOKING TIME: 15 MINS**

6 oz ground turkey
3 green onions, finely chopped
2 tablespoons chopped
   fresh cilantro
1 tablespoon dry sherry
1 tablespoon cornstarch
½ teaspoon Chinese
   five-spice powder
a pinch of salt
2 green onions, thinly sliced, and
   2 teaspoons toasted sesame
   seeds, to serve

FOR THE BROTH
1¼ cups hot chicken stock
2 teaspoons Thai red curry paste
2 teaspoons soy sauce
scant 1 cup coconut cream
4 leaves romaine lettuce, shredded
juice of ½ lime
salt and pepper

Place the turkey, chopped green onions, cilantro, sherry, cornstarch, five-spice powder, and salt in a bowl, and mix well together. Shape the mixture into 12 small balls.

To make the broth, place the stock, curry paste, and soy sauce in a large pan and gently bring to a boil. Season to taste; then add the dumplings and simmer gently for 8–10 minutes until the dumplings are cooked. Stir in the coconut cream, lettuce leaves, and lime juice, and heat gently for 1 minute.

Ladle the broth into serving bowls and sprinkle over the green onions and toasted sesame seeds.

NUTRITION NOTES PER SERVING: calories 517 | protein 25.3 g | carbohydrate 17.1 g fat 38.2 g | saturated fat 30.46 g | fiber 1.6 g | added sugar 0.1 g | salt 1.81 g

lightning coq au vin

We all like a bit of coq au vin once in a while, and mine is well worth remembering, especially as it's ready to eat in lightning time, which is great as, traditionally, this dish is cooked over a long period. Go on, get your coq au vin in.

SERVES 4   PREPARATION: 15 MINS | COOKING TIME: 25 MINS

1 lb 10 oz (750 g) floury
  potatoes, diced
4–5 tablespoons olive oil
6 boneless, skinless chicken
  thighs, halved
1 tablespoon flour,
  seasoned with salt and pepper
8 button onions, quartered
4 slices smoked bacon,
  cut into strips
4 oz (100 g) button
  mushrooms, quartered

1 garlic clove, crushed
2 tablespoons brandy
1¼ cups red wine
2 fresh thyme sprigs or
  ½ teaspoon dried thyme
1 tablespoon tomato paste
½ teaspoon cornstarch
2 tablespoons chopped fresh parsley
salt and pepper

Cook the diced potatoes in a large pan of boiling, salted water for 10–15 minutes until tender. Meanwhile, heat 1 tablespoon of the oil in a large pan. Dust the chicken thighs with seasoned flour and cook in the pan for 1–2 minutes on each side. Add the onions and bacon and cook for 2–3 minutes; then add the mushrooms and garlic and stir-fry for another 2 minutes until well browned. Pour over the brandy and carefully ignite.

When the flames have subsided, pour in the red wine and bring to a boil. Add the thyme and tomato paste, and simmer gently for 15 minutes until the chicken is cooked. Mix the cornstarch to a smooth paste with a little water and stir it in; return to a boil and cook for a minute or so, stirring until thickened. Season to taste.

Drain the potatoes and mash well. Stir in the remaining olive oil and the parsley; season to taste. Divide among the serving plates and spoon over the coq au vin. Serve immediately.

NUTRITION NOTES PER SERVING: calories 592 | protein 29.4 g | carbohydrate 42.8 g fat 27.4 g | saturated fat 7.44 g | fiber 3.7 g | added sugar none | salt 1.52 g

zesty
chick fric

This is just like that old classic, fricassee, and by having the chicken boned, you'll save bags of time. Using thighs keeps the meat juicy, just the way I like it. Why not use the egg whites to make a quick dessert (see page 180)?

SERVES 2 | PREPARATION: 15 MINS | COOKING TIME: 30 MINS

4 boneless chicken thighs
4½ oz (120 g) package boil-in-the-bag basmati rice
2 tablespoons olive oil
1 large onion, thinly sliced
1 carrot, diced
1 celery stalk, roughly diced
1 garlic clove, finely chopped
1 tablespoon all-purpose flour

1¼ cups hot chicken stock
grated rind and juice of 1 lemon
⅓ cup frozen peas
3 egg yolks
2 tablespoons chopped fresh parsley
salt and pepper
quartered lemon slices, to garnish

Heat a heavy-bottomed frying pan. Cut each chicken thigh into 4 pieces and place skin-side down in the frying pan. Cook for 8–10 minutes, turning once, until crisp and golden brown. Cook the rice according to package directions.

Heat the olive oil in a large sauté pan or a frying pan with a lid and cook the onion, carrot, celery, and garlic for 3–4 minutes, stirring until golden. Add the flour to the vegetables, stirring with a wooden spoon, and cook for 1 minute before gradually adding the stock and lemon rind; bring to a boil and then simmer for 3–4 minutes.

Add the chicken to the pan of saucy vegetables, cover and simmer for 3 minutes until the vegetables are tender.

Stir the peas and plenty of salt and pepper into the chicken mixture and cook for 1–2 minutes. Beat the egg yolks; then stir in the lemon juice. Over a gentle heat add the egg yolk mixture to the chicken and stir for a few minutes to thicken the sauce; then stir in the parsley and season to taste.

Spoon the chicken mixture onto a serving plate, garnish with lemon slices, and serve with the rice.

NUTRITION NOTES PER SERVING: calories 862 | protein 40.6 g | carbohydrate 73.4 g fat 47.1 g | saturated fat 11.91 g | fiber 4.9 g | added sugar none | salt 1.11 g

liver and bacon with tsar mash

Some things we like, some things we're not too sure about. Well . . . if you like chicken livers, this recipe will be used again and again and if you're not sure, it's bound to win you over. A real explosive taste that leaves the dishes satisfyingly clean. Buy the chicken livers from your butcher, or check out the freezer section in your supermarket.

SERVES 2 | PREPARATION: 5 MINS | COOKING TIME: 10 MINS

1 lb 2 oz (500 g) potatoes, peeled and diced
1 tablespoon olive oil
4 slices bacon
7 oz (200 g) trimmed chicken livers
1 tablespoon red wine vinegar
2 tablespoons port
⅔ cup sour cream
salt and freshly ground black pepper
snipped chives, to garnish

Cook the potatoes in a large pan of boiling, salted water for 8–10 minutes until tender. Heat the oil in a large frying pan and cook the bacon for 1 minute. Add the chicken livers and cook over a high heat for 1–2 minutes on each side until well browned but still pink in the center; season to taste. Transfer to a heatproof dish and place in the bottom of the oven to keep warm.

Pour the vinegar and port into the hot pan and bubble vigorously for 1 minute. Stir in half the sour cream, lower the heat, and simmer gently for 2–3 minutes until thickened.

Drain the potatoes and return to the pan. Mash well; then beat in the remaining sour cream and season to taste.

Pile the mash onto two serving plates and spoon the liver and bacon on top. Season the sour cream sauce and drizzle over. Garnish with snipped chives and coarsely ground black pepper and serve immediately.

NUTRITION NOTES PER SERVING: calories 756 | protein 33.9 g | carbohydrate 48.3 g
fat 47 g | saturated fat 19.99 g | fiber 3.3 g | added sugar 1.8 g | salt 2.5 g

clever cook's roast chicken dinner

We all have to be pretty crafty in the kitchen at times, and this speedy dinner of roast chicken, honeyed potatoes, bacon-wrapped sausages, stir-fried broccoli, and bread sauce has got me out of hot water on more than one occasion. Y'know that lunch invitation you booked weeks ago but forgot about until the unexpected Sunday 12pm phonecall – "We're on our way?" Help!

SERVES 2 | PREPARATION: 15 MINS | COOKING TIME 25 MINS

4 x 4 oz (100 g) potatoes, each halved lengthwise
2 x 4 oz (100 g) boneless chicken breasts
a large knob of butter
2 slices smoked bacon
4 sausages
1 small onion, finely chopped
⅔ cup milk

¾ cup fresh white breadcrumbs
a pinch of ground nutmeg
1 tablespoon clear honey
2 tablespoons olive oil
1 garlic clove, thinly sliced
7 oz (200 g) broccoli florets
salt and pepper

Preheat the oven to 425°F (220°C). Cook the potatoes in a large pan of boiling, salted water for 10–15 minutes until just tender. Meanwhile, place the chicken breasts in a roasting pan, season well and dot with a little butter. Roast in the oven for 25 minutes until golden brown and cooked through. Meanwhile, stretch the bacon with the back of a knife and cut each slice in half widthwise. Wrap a half slice around each sausage and add to the chicken pan.

Heat the remaining butter in a small pan and cook the onion for 3–4 minutes until softened; then pour in the milk and bring to a boil. Lower the heat and stir in the breadcrumbs and nutmeg; season to taste and keep warm.

Drain the potatoes and return to the pan. Toss with the honey and 1 tablespoon of the oil and arrange around the chicken in the roasting pan. Return to the oven for 8–10 minutes until golden brown. Heat the remaining oil in a wok and stir-fry the garlic and broccoli for 2 minutes. Add a splash of water and cook for another 2 minutes until tender. Season to taste. Place the chicken breasts on large serving plates with the honeyed potatoes, bacon-wrapped sausages, stir-fried broccoli, and bread sauce.

NUTRITION NOTES PER SERVING: calories 919 | protein 45.5 g | carbohydrate 73.8 g fat 51 g | saturated fat 17.91 g | fiber 6.5 g | added sugar 9.6 g | salt 3.11 g

acapulco chicken

An idea created from lots of left-over broken tortilla chips and now a family favorite. Even friends request it when coming over for a casual supper. One teaspoon of chile if you like it hot, two if you like it hot, hot, hot. Can you feel it?

SERVES 4   **PREPARATION: 10 MINS | COOKING TIME: 30 MINS**

1 tablespoon vegetable oil
8 boneless, skinless chicken thighs, cut into chunks
1 onion, sliced
2 garlic cloves, chopped
1–2 teaspoons chile powder, plus extra for sprinkling
1 x 14 oz (400 g) can chopped tomatoes
¾ cup chicken stock
1 x 14 oz (400 g) can kidney beans, drained
½ teaspoon dried oregano
4 oz (100 g) tortilla chips
salt and pepper
sour cream and parsley sprigs, to garnish
cooked rice, to serve

Heat the oil in a pan, add the chicken, onion, and garlic, and cook for about 5 minutes until golden. Add the chile and stir-fry for 30 seconds; then add the tomatoes, stock, kidney beans, and oregano. Season with salt and pepper. Bring to a boil, cover and simmer for 20 minutes, or until the chicken is tender.

Transfer the chicken to a serving dish and sprinkle over the tortilla chips. Top with a dollop of sour cream, some parsley sprigs, and a sprinkling of chile powder. Serve with rice.

NUTRITION NOTES PER SERVING: calories 596 | protein 31 g | carbohydrate 52 g
fat 31 g | saturated fat 7 g | fiber 7 g | added sugar none | salt 1.95 g

cha-cha-cha chimichangas

Chimichangas are simply fried Mexican tortillas. That'll get you cha-cha-cha-ing around your kitchen.

SERVES 4 | PREPARATION: 15 MINS | COOKING TIME: 15 MINS

sunflower oil, for frying
1 onion, finely chopped
1 red bell pepper, seeded and diced
2 boneless, skinless chicken thighs, roughly chopped
2 green chiles, seeded and thinly sliced
2 garlic cloves, finely chopped
2 tomatoes, roughly chopped
½ cup frozen corn, thawed
4 tablespoons taco sauce
4 green onions, finely chopped
4 large flour tortillas
shredded lettuce, sour cream, and ready-made guacamole, to serve

Heat the sunflower oil in a large pan and stir-fry the onion, bell pepper, and chicken thighs over a high heat for 3–4 minutes until well browned. Stir in the chiles, garlic, tomatoes, and corn, and cook for another 2–3 minutes until the chicken is cooked through.

Stir in the taco sauce and green onions, and set aside to cool a little.

Warm one of the tortillas in a hot, dry frying pan until soft and flexible. Spoon a quarter of the cooled chicken mixture into the center of the tortilla and fold over the edges to form a neat package; pin in place with wooden toothpicks and repeat with the remaining tortillas.

Heat ½ inch (1 cm) vegetable oil in a large frying pan and cook the chimichangas for 2–3 minutes on each side until crisp and golden brown. Drain on paper towels and serve hot with shredded lettuce, sour cream, and guacamole.

NUTRITION NOTES PER SERVING: calories 374 | protein 12.8 g | carbohydrate 38.2 g fat 19.9 g | saturated fat 3.01 g | fiber 3.1 g | added sugar none | salt 0.42 g

sos chicken with pilau rice

"S" for succulent, "O" for orgasmic, "S" for saucy; and all this in just 15 minutes. Ooh, you lucky people.

SERVES 4 | PREPARATION: 5 MINS | COOKING TIME: 10 MINS

2¼ cups tomato purée
1–2 tablespoons hot curry paste
1 lb 2 oz (500 g) cooked boneless
   tandoori or tikka chicken breasts
   or thighs, cut into bite-size pieces
⅔ cup heavy cream
½ teaspoon superfine sugar
salt and pepper

FOR THE RICE
1 tablespoon vegetable oil
1 onion, sliced
¼ cup slivered almonds
2½ cups cooked white rice
1 teaspoon ground turmeric
2 tablespoons seedless raisins
salt and pepper
chopped fresh cilantro,
   to garnish (optional)

Place the tomato purée in a small pan, stir in the curry paste, and heat gently.

Meanwhile, for the rice, heat the oil in a wok and stir-fry the onion for 2 minutes; add the almonds and cook for another 2 minutes until both are nicely browned. Stir in the rice, turmeric, and raisins, and heat gently for 3–4 minutes, adding a splash of water if the mixture is a little dry.

Add the chicken and cream to the tomato mixture, bring to a boil and simmer for 2 minutes until warmed through. Stir in the sugar and season to taste.

Season the rice and divide between serving plates. Spoon over the chicken and garnish with cilantro, if using.

NUTRITION NOTES PER SERVING: calories 687 | protein 44.5 g | carbohydrate 55.8 g fat 33.2 g | saturated fat 14.13 g | fiber 2.8 g | added sugar 4.4 g | salt 1.3 g

I make this using left-over rice, but cooked rice is now available in free-flow frozen form or in cans.

gorgeous
chicken korma

My chicken korma is based on a spicy, creamy dish from Kashmir. It's incredibly easy to make and very, very tasty. Chicken korma is popular because the flavors blend together perfectly, leaving that gorgeous taste lingering on your tastebuds 'til the next mouthful.

SERVES 4 | **PREPARATION: 10 MINS | COOKING TIME: 30 MINS**

1 tablespoon vegetable oil
1 onion, roughly chopped
1½ cups plain yogurt
scant 1 cup heavy cream
2 tablespoons butter
½ teaspoon salt
1 teaspoon ground turmeric
2 teaspoons hot chile powder
3 garlic cloves, crushed

3 tablespoons ground almonds
4 x 4 oz (100 g) boneless,
   skinless chicken breasts, each
   cut into six pieces
toasted slivered almonds and
   fresh cilantro sprigs,
   to garnish (optional)
naan bread or rice, and cucumber
   and red onion salad, to serve

Preheat the oven to 400°F (200°C).

Heat the oil in a small pan and cook the onion for 5 minutes until softened. Place in a food processor with the yogurt, cream, butter, salt, turmeric, chile, garlic, and almonds, and whizz until well blended.

Arrange the chicken in a greased casserole and pour over the korma mixture. Bake for 30 minutes until the chicken is cooked through. Spoon onto plates, garnish with slivered almonds and cilantro sprigs, if you wish, and serve with naan or rice and salad.

NUTRITION NOTES PER SERVING: calories 549 | protein 30.4 g | carbohydrate 11.8 g fat 42.7 g | saturated fat 20.85 g | fiber 1.4 g | added sugar none | salt 1.19 g

If you have time, let the chicken marinade in the korma sauce for up to 2 hours before cooking.

doodle spinach 'n'chicken noodle

This succulent and nutritious dish, with a hint of the Orient, cooks in a flash and tastes divine. If you've got greens instead of spinach, that'll do fine.

SERVES 2 | **PREPARATION: 10 MINS | COOKING TIME: 10 MINS**

6 oz (175 g) egg noodles
1 tablespoon sunflower oil
2 small boneless, skinless chicken breasts, thinly sliced diagonally
1 bunch green onions, trimmed and halved widthwise
1 garlic clove, sliced
4 oz (100 g) chestnut mushrooms, sliced
1½ teaspoons coarsely crushed black peppercorns
3 tablespoons oyster sauce
scant ½ cup chicken stock
4 oz (100 g) spinach leaves, cut into large strips (remove any tough stalks)
salt and pepper

Cook the noodles in boiling water for about 4 minutes, or according to the package directions. Drain well and keep warm.

Meanwhile, heat the sunflower oil in a frying pan; then add the chicken slices, season and cook over a high heat for 3–4 minutes until browned and almost cooked through. Add the green onions, garlic, mushrooms, and crushed peppercorns to the pan, and cook, stirring, for 2 minutes.

Add the oyster sauce and stock to the pan, stirring to heat through. Add the spinach leaves and cook for 1–2 minutes until just wilted. Stir and season with salt; then serve on a bed of noodles.

NUTRITION NOTES PER SERVING: calories 562 | protein 37 g | carbohydrate 70 g
fat 17 g | saturated fat 2 g | fiber 5 g | added sugar none | salt 3.81 g

ginger chicken with coconut rice

The delicious smells coming from the oven once this is on the go will drive your family's tastebuds wild.

SERVES 4	PREPARATION: 10 MINS | COOKING TIME: 25 MINS

1 tablespoon vegetable oil
4 boneless chicken breasts, unskinned
2 tablespoons clear honey
1 tablespoon dark soy sauce
2 garlic cloves, crushed
a ¾ inch (2 cm) piece of ginger root, finely grated
grated rind and juice of 1 large orange
8 oz (225 g) button mushrooms, halved
2 bunches green onions, trimmed and halved
a 2 oz (50 g) block creamed coconut, roughly chopped
generous 1 cup long-grain rice
1 bay leaf
orange wedges and bay leaves, to garnish

Preheat the oven to 375°F (190°C).

Heat the oil in a frying pan and cook the chicken, skin-side down, for 2–3 minutes on each side until golden brown; transfer to an ovenproof dish. Mix together the honey, soy sauce, garlic, ginger, and orange rind and juice, and pour over the chicken. Bake for 10 minutes; then add the mushrooms and green onions, baste and bake for another 10 minutes.

Meanwhile, make the coconut rice: bring 1¾ cups of water to a boil in a nonstick pan, add the creamed coconut, and stir until it is dissolved; add the rice and bay leaf, cover and simmer for 12–15 minutes, stirring occasionally, until the rice is tender and the liquid absorbed. Serve with the chicken, garnished with orange wedges and bay leaves.

NUTRITION NOTES PER SERVING: calories 484 | protein 34 g | carbohydrate 56 g
fat 16 g | saturated fat 9 g | fiber 3 g | added sugar 8 g | salt 0.27 g

flash
chicken satay

I always serve chicken satay (the miniature variety) before we get down to the serious nosh, and the plate is empty in a flash. These scrummy skewers make a great main course and are also delicious cooked over hot coals and served with a cold beer.

SERVES 2 | PREPARATION: 15 MINS | COOKING TIME: 10 MINS

scant 1 cup coconut cream
4 tablespoons crunchy
  peanut butter
1–2 teaspoons
  Worcestershire sauce
a few drops of Tabasco sauce
2 x 3 oz (75 g) boneless,
  skinless chicken breasts

1 lemon
1 carrot, cut into thin ribbons
1 mini cucumber,
  cut into thin ribbons
salt and pepper
¼ cup dry-roasted
  peanuts, roughly chopped, and
  2 warm naan breads, to serve

Preheat the oven to 400°F (200°C). Preheat the broiler to high.

Place the coconut cream and peanut butter in a bowl and beat together until well blended. Stir in the Worcestershire sauce and Tabasco. Sandwich the chicken breasts between plastic wrap; then, using a rolling pin, bat them out as thinly as possible. Remove the plastic wrap and cut each breast in half lengthwise.

Pour half the sauce into a shallow dish and add the chicken pieces, turning to coat them in the sauce. Thread onto skewers and cook under a hot broiler for 4 minutes, or on each side until cooked through and well browned.

Gently heat the reserved satay sauce with a splash of water in a small pan. Place the naan in the oven to warm through.

Halve the lemon and squeeze the juice of one half into the warm satay sauce. Pile the carrot and cucumber ribbons on top of the warm naans and squeeze over the remaining lemon juice. Arrange the skewers on top and drizzle over the warm satay sauce.

NUTRITION NOTES PER SERVING: calories 1090 | protein 44.6 g | carbohydrate 80.4 g fat 66 g | saturated fat 33.79 g | fiber 5.7 g | added sugar 0.7 g | salt 2.15 g

chester's chicken chow mein

You can throw this together much quicker than the time it takes to get to the local take-out and back, and it tastes every bit as good. It's one of my dad's favorites, and he's always flabbergasted at how little time it takes – "But you only just went to the kitchen!"

SERVES 2 | PREPARATION: 5 MINS | COOKING TIME: 10 MINS

6 oz (175 g) egg noodles
1 tablespoon sunflower oil
1 onion, thinly sliced
2 garlic cloves, thinly sliced
a ½ inch (1 cm) piece of ginger root, finely chopped (optional)
4 oz (100 g) beansprouts
4 oz (100 g) snow peas, halved lengthwise, or peas
1¼ cups shredded cooked chicken
1 tablespoon soy sauce
1 tablespoon sweet chile sauce

Cook the noodles in a large pan of boiling, salted water, according to the package directions. Meanwhile, heat the oil in a wok or deep frying pan and stir-fry the onion over a high heat for 2–3 minutes until beginning to brown. Add the garlic, ginger (if using), beansprouts, and snow peas or peas and stir-fry for 1 minute.

Drain the noodles well and add to the wok with the chicken and soy sauce; cook for 2 minutes until piping hot. Stir in the sweet chile sauce and serve immediately.

NUTRITION NOTES PER SERVING: calories 616 | protein 41.2 g | carbohydrate 73.2 g fat 19.6 g | saturated fat 2.9 g | fiber 5.5 g | added sugar none | salt 1.69 g

chiang mai thai bolognese

This puts a spicy spin on the traditional bolognese. For extra authenticity, serve with Thai fragrant rice.

SERVES 4	PREPARATION: 10 MINS | COOKING TIME: 15 MINS

1⅓ cups long-grain or Thai fragrant rice
1 tablespoon vegetable oil
1 onion, halved and sliced
1 garlic clove, chopped
1 red bell pepper, cored, seeded and roughly chopped
1 lb (450 g) ground turkey or pork
½ teaspoon chile powder
2 tablespoons dark soy sauce
¾ cup chicken stock
2 teaspoons cornstarch
a handful of fresh basil leaves
salt and pepper

Cook the rice in a pan of boiling water for about 15 minutes. Meanwhile, heat the oil in a pan and cook the onion for 3–4 minutes until golden. Stir in the garlic and bell pepper, and cook for 4 minutes; then add the ground turkey or pork and chile powder and cook for 2–3 minutes until well browned. Stir in the soy sauce and stock, bring to a boil, and simmer for 5 minutes.

Blend the cornstarch with 1 tablespoon of water until smooth, add to the pan, and stir until slightly thickened. Season with pepper and stir in the whole basil leaves. Drain the rice and spoon onto plates; top with the bolognese and serve.

NUTRITION NOTES PER SERVING: calories 413 \| protein 30 g \| carbohydrate 63 g
fat 6 g \| saturated fat 1 g \| fiber 1 g \| added sugar none \| salt 0.33 g

For a richer taste, stir in 1 tablespoon of oyster sauce with the soy sauce and stock.

prosciutto turkey roulades

Turkey escalopes are delicious when wrapped in prosciutto – in fact, any cured ham will do, or you could even use thinly sliced smoked bacon.

SERVES 4 | **PREPARATION: 10 MINS | COOKING TIME 10 MINS**

4 x 5 oz (150 g) turkey escalopes
2 garlic cloves, finely chopped
grated rind and juice of 1 lemon
2 tablespoons chopped fresh basil or chives
4 slices prosciutto
2 tablespoons olive oil
salt and pepper
mixed salad and freshly cooked pasta or crusty Italian bread, to serve

Halve each turkey escalope horizontally and open out. Season the flesh well and sprinkle over the garlic, lemon rind, and chopped herbs; then sandwich the pieces back together again. Wrap each escalope in a slice of prosciutto and pin in place with wooden toothpicks.

Heat the olive oil in a frying pan and cook the turkey for 4–5 minutes until golden brown. Turn over, drizzle with the lemon juice, and cook for another 3–4 minutes until cooked through. Serve with salad and pasta or warm, crusty, sun-dried tomato bread.

NUTRITION NOTES PER SERVING: calories 261 | protein 42.8 g | carbohydrate 0.7 g fat 9.6 g | saturated fat 2.22 g | fiber 0.1 g | added sugar none | salt 1.62 g

peking
duck

When I go to a Chinese restaurant I particularly enjoy the sociability involved in eating Peking duck. It was a real challenge coming up with a quick version, as it normally takes hours to prepare.

SERVES 2 | **PREPARATION: 10 MINS | COOKING TIME 10 MINS**

2 x 6 oz (175 g) duck breasts
1 tablespoon dark soy sauce
2 tablespoons clear honey
1 teaspoon Chinese five-
    spice powder
¼ teaspoon coarse black pepper
1 tablespoon sunflower oil

FOR THE PLUM SAUCE
1 teaspoon sesame oil
1 garlic clove, crushed
1 tablespoon white wine vinegar

1 tablespoon soy sauce
3 tablespoons plum jam
a pinch of dried chile flakes

TO SERVE
10 Chinese-style
    pancakes, warmed
4 green onions, shredded
a 4 inch (10 cm) piece of cucumber,
    cut into matchsticks
2 tablespoons fresh cilantro
    leaves, plus sprigs, to serve

Halve the duck breasts horizontally; then cut each piece lengthwise into very thin strips. Stir together the soy sauce, honey, five-spice powder, and pepper; pour over the duck and set aside to marinate for a few minutes. Meanwhile, heat the sesame oil in a small pan and gently cook the garlic for 1 minute without coloring; then stir in the vinegar, soy sauce, jam, and chile flakes. Cook for 2 minutes, stirring until well blended and warmed through. Pass the sauce through a fine sieve into a small serving dish. Drain the duck strips. Heat the sunflower oil in a wok or deep frying pan and stir-fry the duck over a high heat for 2–3 minutes until well browned. To serve, spread the warm pancakes with a little of the plum sauce and top with a few strips of duck, green onion, and cucumber. Sprinkle over some cilantro leaves and roll up. Garnish with cilantro sprigs and serve.

NUTRITION NOTES PER SERVING: calories 1139 | protein 26.3 g | carbohydrate 52.9 g
fat 92.8 g | saturated fat 26.4 g | fiber 1.2 g | added sugar 34.7 g | salt 2.83 g

To warm the pancakes through, place them on a heatproof plate, cover with foil and sit over a pan of gently simmering water for 4–5 minutes.

succulent spiced duckling

This is a very stylish meal, perfect for special occasions – it looks impressive but is really simple to make. It goes down beautifully with a nice spicy red wine.

SERVES 2	PREPARATION: 15 MINS	COOKING TIME: 25 MINS

2 x 4 oz (100 g) duckling breasts
1 teaspoon mixed spice
½ teaspoon cayenne pepper
½ teaspoon salt

FOR THE CABBAGE
a knob of butter
8 oz (225 g) red cabbage, shredded
1 small red onion, thinly sliced
1 tart apple, peeled and diced

2 tablespoons light
  raw brown sugar
¼ teaspoon ground cinnamon
½ cup red wine
juice of 1 orange
4 tablespoons sour cream
a handful of chopped fresh herbs,
  such as basil, parsley, cilantro,
  chives
salt and pepper

Score the duck skin in a lattice pattern. Mix the spices and salt in a shallow bowl and add the duck; using your fingertips, rub in the spices.

Cook the duck skin-side down in a hot griddle pan or frying pan for 7 minutes on each side until browned and cooked through but still a little pink in the center. Remove from the pan and place on a warm plate to rest for 5 minutes.

Meanwhile, melt the butter in a wok or deep frying pan and stir-fry the cabbage over a high heat for 1–2 minutes. Add the red onion and apple, and cook for another 1–2 minutes. Stir in the sugar and cinnamon, and cook, stirring, until the sugar dissolves. Add the wine and orange juice, and simmer gently for 10 minutes until tender.

Meanwhile, stir together the sour cream and fresh herbs, and season to taste. Spoon the cabbage onto serving plates. Slice the duck breasts and fan out on top of the cabbage, top with a spoonful of herby cream, and serve immediately.

NUTRITION NOTES PER SERVING: calories 674 | protein 14.7 g | carbohydrate 25 g fat 53.5 g | saturated fat 18.03 g | fiber 4.7 g | added sugar 5.2 | salt 1.85 g

POULTRY

poetry meat the pla

131	SPICED SHISH SKEWERS	30 MINS
133	LAZY LUSCIOUS LAMB BIRYANI	30 MINS
134	SNAPPY LAMB HOT POT	40 MINS
137	JOY SOY LAMB AND GINGER RICE	40 MINS
138	JAZZ AND SPICE SHEPHERD'S PIE	30 MINS
140	BROILED PEPPERY PORK AND APPLE	20 MINS
141	CANTON STIR-FRIED BEEF WITH NOODLES	15 MINS
142	JOE'S BAKE AND GLAZE STICKY RIBS	50 MINS
144	SPICE BRIT'S PORK CHOP CHOW	30 MINS
145	CHILE-JAM HAM STEAKS	30 MINS
147	FRENCH-STYLE PORK WITH ROOT PURÉE	25 MINS
148	PASTA CREAM BEAN DREAM	20 MINS
151	MARVELOUS CHILE-CHEESE MEATBALLS	30 MINS
152	PAVAROTTI PASTA	20 MINS
155	MY MADDIE'S SPICY SAUSAGES	30 MINS
156	DOUBLE-QUICK CAROLINE'S CASSOULET	50 MINS
158	MUSTARD BASIL BEEF ROLLS	25 MINS
159	BEEFBURGERS WITH BLUE CHEESE SAUCE	20 MINS
161	PEPPERED NUGGET STEAK	30 MINS

spiced
shish skewers

I bet you can't say that after a few glasses of wine! As for the dip, it's simply a combination of cucumber and tomato, but that doesn't sound half as exciting or sexy as it tastes. This dish is also super served cold.

SERVES 4 | **PREPARATION: 15 MINS | COOKING TIME: 15 MINS**

1 lb ground lamb
1 small onion, finely chopped
3 tablespoons chopped fresh mint
1 tablespoon each chopped fresh oregano and parsley
½ teaspoon each mixed spice, ground coriander, and ground cumin
1 lb (450 g) small new potatoes
½ small cucumber
⅔ cup plain yogurt
1 tomato, seeded and diced
¼ teaspoon garlic powder or 1 garlic clove, crushed
salt and pepper
4 pita breads, plus wedges of cucumber, tomato, and lemon, to serve

Preheat the broiler to high. Mix together the lamb, onion, 1 tablespoon of mint, the oregano, parsley, mixed spice, coriander, and cumin; and season with salt and pepper. Divide the mixture into 12 and squeeze around 12 skewers.

Cook the potatoes in boiling, salted water for 10–15 minutes or until tender.

Broil the lamb kebabs for 8–10 minutes, turning occasionally until well browned. Meanwhile, grate the cucumber, squeeze out the excess liquid with your hands, and mix with the yogurt, tomato, 1 tablespoon of mint, the garlic, and salt and pepper.

Drain the potatoes and toss with the remaining mint. Serve the lamb with potatoes, pita bread, a dollop of the yogurt, and wedges of fresh cucumber and tomato. Oh – and a wedge of lemon, too!

NUTRITION NOTES PER SERVING: calories 393 | protein 25 g | carbohydrate 25 g fat 22 g | saturated fat 11 g | fiber 2 g | added sugar none | salt 0.52 g

lazy luscious lamb biryani

The classic biryani is a festive casserole of rice and meat. Traditionally, the grains of rice are yellow and white, the yellow provided by saffron mixed with milk, then drizzled over the top of the rice before cooking. If you're feeling posh, why not replace the turmeric with a few strands of saffron – the cooking aroma and taste are exceptional.

SERVES 4 | PREPARATION: 10 MINS | COOKING TIME: 20 MINS

1 teaspoon each ground
  turmeric and cumin
½ teaspoon each ground
  coriander and chile powder
2 tablespoons vegetable oil
9 oz (250 g) lean, boneless
  lamb, cubed
1 tablespoon butter
1 onion, sliced
2 garlic cloves, chopped

1 cinnamon stick, halved
1¼ cups basmati rice
2½ cups hot chicken
  or vegetable stock
12 oz (350 g) small
  cauliflower florets
⅔ cup peas
salt and pepper
toasted slivered almonds, to garnish

Mix together the turmeric, cumin, coriander, chile, and 1 tablespoon of the oil. Toss the lamb in the mixture to coat.

Heat the butter and remaining oil in a pan and cook the onion and garlic for 4–5 minutes until softened. Add the cinnamon and lamb, and cook over a high heat for 3 minutes.

Stir in the rice and stock, and bring to a boil. Add the cauliflower, cover and simmer gently for 8–10 minutes until the rice is almost tender. Stir in the peas and cook for another 2–3 minutes until the stock has been absorbed. Remove the cinnamon stick, season to taste, and serve garnished with the toasted slivered almonds.

NUTRITION NOTES PER SERVING: calories 459 | protein 23.7 g | carbohydrate 55 g
fat 17.5 g | saturated fat 5.41 g | fiber 3.5 g | added sugar none | salt 0.99 g

snappy lamb hot pot

In northern England the hot pot was a tall, earthenware pot. Mutton chops were stacked round the sides, the veggies in the middle, and a dozen oysters were slipped in on special occasions before it was finished off with a layer of sliced potatoes and baked for two to three hours. But with my version you really can cook a delicious, classic hot pot in less than a half-hour.

SERVES 4　　PREPARATION: 15 MINS | COOKING TIME 25 MINS

4 x 4 oz (100 g) trimmed
　lean lamb steaks
2 tablespoons olive oil
1 onion, sliced
1 garlic clove, sliced
14 oz (400 g) can
　chopped tomatoes
½ cup hot chicken or
　vegetable stock

4 oz (100 g) green beans, halved
½ teaspoon mixed dried herbs
a few drops of Tabasco or chile
　sauce
1 lb 2 oz (500 g) parboiled
　potatoes, very thinly sliced
a knob of butter
salt and pepper

Cut each piece of lamb lengthwise into two or three strips. Heat the oil in a large sauté pan or a frying pan with a lid and cook the onion, garlic, and lamb for 3–4 minutes until well browned.

Stir in the tomatoes, stock, beans, and herbs, and bring to a boil; add Tabasco, salt and pepper to taste.

Arrange the potatoes in overlapping layers on top of the meat. Season, cover and simmer for 15 minutes until the potato is tender.

Preheat the broiler to high. Dot the potatoes with butter and place under the broiler for 2–3 minutes until nicely browned.

NUTRITION NOTES PER SERVING: calories 355 | protein 25.2 g | carbohydrate 27.7 g
fat 16.8 g | saturated fat 6.29 g | fiber 3.3 g | added sugar none | salt 0.93 g

To parboil potatoes, cook them whole, or halved if they are large, in a pan of boiling water for 10 minutes, or until they are almost tender. Drain and cool before continuing with the recipe.

joy soy lamb and ginger rice

I'm particularly fond of lamb. Perhaps it's something to do with its subtle sweetness. This dish is full of Oriental flavors and style.

SERVES 4 | **PREPARATION: 10 MINS | COOKING TIME: 30 MINS**

1 teaspoon ground fennel or cumin

1 garlic clove, crushed

1 tablespoon chopped fresh rosemary, or 1 teaspoon dried rosemary

1 teaspoon each grated lemon rind and juice

3 tablespoons olive oil

1 tablespoon soy sauce

1 onion, sliced

2 garlic cloves, finely chopped

¾ inch (2 cm) of ginger root, finely chopped

generous 1 cup long-grain rice

4 oz (100 g) button mushrooms, sliced

2 cups hot vegetable stock

½ teaspoon ground turmeric

4 x 4 oz (100 g) boneless rump, leg or shoulder lamb steaks

2 tablespoons chopped fresh cilantro or parsley

salt and pepper

½ cucumber, seeded and cut into strips, to garnish

Stir together the fennel or cumin, garlic, rosemary, lemon rind and juice, 2 tablespoons of the oil, and the soy sauce; set aside.

Heat the remaining oil in a pan and cook the onion, garlic, and ginger for 4–5 minutes until softened and golden. Stir in the rice and cook, stirring, for 1 minute. Add the mushrooms, stock, and turmeric, and bring to a boil. Cover and simmer gently for 15 minutes until the liquid is absorbed and the rice is tender.

Preheat the broiler to high. Brush the lamb with the soy sauce mix, then broil for 4 minutes; turn, brush with more soy sauce mixture and cook for 3–4 minutes longer until crispy and tender. Stir the cilantro or parsley into the rice and season. Spoon the rice onto serving plates, slice the lamb into strips, and arrange on top of the rice. Garnish with fine strips of cucumber.

NUTRITION NOTES PER SERVING: calories 527 | protein 23.1 g | carbohydrate 48.5 g fat 28.1 g | saturated fat 10.67 g | fiber 0.9 g | added sugar none | salt 1.31 g

MEAT

jazz and spice shepherd's pie

Shepherd's pie is such a lovely old-fashioned dish – here I've jazzed it up to great effect with a touch of spicy curry paste.

SERVES 2-3 | PREPARATION: 10 MINS | COOKING TIME: 20 MINS

1 lb (450 g) floury potatoes, diced
2 tablespoons sunflower oil
1 small onion, finely chopped
1 garlic clove, finely chopped
1 large carrot, diced
10 oz ground lamb
2 tablespoons mild curry paste
1 cup hot lamb stock
1 tablespoon tomato ketchup

2 teaspoons dark soy sauce
1 teaspoon cornstarch
⅓ cup frozen peas, thawed
2 tomatoes, roughly chopped
2 tablespoons milk
a knob of butter
¼ cup grated sharp Cheddar
salt and pepper

Cook the potatoes in a large pan of boiling, salted water for 8–10 minutes until tender.

Heat 1 tablespoon of sunflower oil in a large frying pan and cook the onion, garlic, carrot, and ground lamb for 3–4 minutes until well browned. Stir in the curry paste, stock, tomato ketchup, and soy sauce. Bring to a boil and simmer rapidly for 3–4 minutes. Mix the cornstarch to a paste with a little water and stir into the pan with the peas and chopped tomatoes; bring back to a boil, stirring, until slightly thickened. Season with salt and pepper to taste.

Drain the potatoes well and return to the pan. Mash well, then beat in the milk and butter until smooth and creamy; season to taste.

Preheat the broiler to medium. Spoon the lamb mixture into a heatproof pie dish and spoon over the mashed potato. Using a fork, mark a criss-cross pattern on the top.

Sprinkle over the Cheddar and place under a medium broiler for 3 minutes until the cheese melts and the pie is speckled with brown. Spoon onto plates and serve.

NUTRITION NOTES PER SERVING: calories 864 | protein 40.6 g | carbohydrate 60.4 g
fat 52.6 g | saturated fat 21.87 g | fiber 10.6 g | added sugar 1 g | salt 2.08 g

broiled peppery pork and apple

Perk up your pork with my peppery coating.

SERVES 4   PREPARATION: 10 MINS | COOKING TIME: 10 MINS

14 oz (400 g) pork fillet, cut into 12 x ¾ inch (2 cm) thick slices
1½ teaspoons freshly ground black pepper
½ teaspoon paprika
grated rind of 1 lemon
1 teaspoon fresh lemon juice
4 tablespoons olive oil
2 apples, unpeeled
10 oz (300 g) savoy cabbage, finely shredded
1 garlic clove, finely chopped
⅔ cup vegetable stock
scant 1 cup crème fraîche
salt and pepper

Preheat the broiler to high. Place the pork slices between two layers of plastic wrap; then press down with the palm of your hand to flatten the meat out to a thickness of about ¼ inch (6 mm). Remove the plastic wrap.

In a bowl, mix together the pepper, paprika, lemon rind and juice, and 3 tablespoons of the oil. Slice each apple widthwise into four slices. Drizzle the oil mixture over one side of the pork and apple slices. Broil the pork slices for 4–5 minutes on each side, turning once. Broil the apple slices, on the oiled side only, for about 5 minutes until cooked. Keep the pork and apple slices warm.

Meanwhile, heat the remaining oil in a large frying pan. Add the cabbage and garlic, and cook, covered, for 4–5 minutes until just tender. Stir in the stock and the crème fraîche, warm through briefly, and season to taste; then spoon onto warmed serving plates. Top with the pork slices and serve the apple slices on the side or on top.

NUTRITION NOTES PER SERVING: calories 454 | protein 23 g | carbohydrate 14 g
fat 34 g | saturated fat 14 g | fiber 3 g | added sugar none | salt 1.08 g

canton stir-fried beef with noodles

What came first – Chinese noodles or Italian spaghetti? The argument will go on for another 100 years. This Cantonese dish is one of the quickest and tastiest around – guaranteed to have you wok-ing. Yes, owright Ainsley . . .

SERVES 2 | PREPARATION: 10 MINS | COOKING TIME: 5 MINS

9 oz (250 g) tender beef steak cut into ½ inch (1 cm) wide strips
1 tablespoon soy sauce
1 tablespoon dry sherry
1 tablespoon hoisin sauce
2 tablespoons cornstarch
2 tablespoons sunflower oil, plus extra for deep frying
1 oz (25 g) cellophane (sometimes labeled "stir-fry" noodles) or rice noodles
4 oz (100g) bok choy leaves or broccoli florets

1 red bell pepper, seeded and sliced
a handful of fresh basil leaves, roughly torn
salt and pepper

FOR THE SAUCE
4 tablespoons dry sherry
2 tablespoons light soy sauce
1 teaspoon sesame oil
1 tablespoon clear honey
1 teaspoon hot chile sauce
cooked Thai-style fragrant rice, to serve

Place the beef strips in a bowl with the soy sauce, sherry, hoisin sauce, and cornstarch; mix well and set aside. Deep fry the noodles in hot oil for 30 seconds until puffed and white. Remove with a slotted spoon and drain on paper towels.

To make the sauce stir together the sherry, soy sauce, sesame oil, honey, and hot chile sauce. Heat a little oil in a wok and stir-fry the beef, making sure you add the juices from the marinade, too, for 1 minute. Add the bok choy and bell pepper, and cook for 2 minutes. Add the sauce and cook for another 2 minutes until the meat is tender; stir in the basil and check the seasoning.

Divide the rice between two serving plates and spoon over the spicy beef mixture. Top with the crispy noodles and serve immediately.

NUTRITION NOTES PER SERVING: calories 698 | protein 29.3 g | carbohydrate 58.1 g
fat 35.6 g | saturated fat 5.97 g | fiber 1.9 g | added sugar 12.3 g | salt 1.86 g

MEAT

joe's bake and glaze sticky ribs

A good, quick recipe for spareribs that my nephew Joe always insists on when he comes to supper. He loves the sucking, licking and picking of these sticky ribs. Time to get glazing! PS Serve with plenty of paper napkins.

SERVES 4 PREPARATION: 10 MINS | COOKING TIME 40 MINS

2¼ lb (1 kg) pork spareribs
1 onion, sliced
1 teaspoon dried mixed herbs
5 tablespoons tomato ketchup
3 tablespoons apple or orange juice
⅔ cup dark raw brown sugar
1 tablespoon English mustard
3 tablespoons Worcestershire sauce
½–1 teaspoon Tabasco sauce
1¼ lb (550 g) potatoes, cut into wedges
1 tablespoon olive oil
salt and pepper
mixed salad leaves and cherry tomato halves, to serve

Preheat the oven to 400°F (200°C). Place the ribs, onion, and herbs in a large pan and cover with water. Bring to a boil; then lower the heat and simmer for 20 minutes.

Meanwhile, in a bowl, mix the tomato ketchup, fruit juice, sugar, mustard, Worcestershire and Tabasco sauces, and salt and pepper. Steam the potatoes for 10 minutes.

Using a slotted spoon, place the spareribs in a single layer in a shallow ovenproof dish and spoon over the glaze. Place the potatoes on a baking sheet, brush with olive oil and season. Bake the meat and potatoes for 20 minutes, or until the meat is tender and the potatoes crisp. Serve with salad leaves and cherry tomatoes.

NUTRITION NOTES PER SERVING: calories 849 | protein 30 g | carbohydrate 53 g
fat 59 g | saturated fat 23 g | fiber 2 g | added sugar 22 g | salt 1.11 g

spice brit's pork chop chow

Succulent pork with fresh beet chutney and creamy garlic potatoes. This combination works so well that you'll be getting requests for a repeat performance.

SERVES 4 | PREPARATION: 10 MINS | COOKING TIME: 20 MINS

1 lb (450g) small new potatoes
2 tablespoons butter
1 onion, chopped
1½ cups coarsely grated cooked beets
2 tablespoons cider vinegar
½ teaspoon ground ginger
grated rind and juice of 1 orange
2 tablespoons raisins

2 teaspoons light raw brown sugar
4 x 5 oz (150 g) pork loin chops with bone
1 teaspoon English mustard
6 tablespoons heavy cream
1 garlic clove, crushed
1 tablespoon snipped fresh chives
salt and pepper

Cook the potatoes in lightly salted boiling water for 15 minutes or until tender. Meanwhile, melt the butter in a pan, add the onion, and cook for 3–4 minutes until golden. Stir in the beets, vinegar, ginger, the orange rind and juice, raisins, and sugar. Cover and simmer for 5 minutes, or until softened.

Preheat the broiler to high. Season the chops and brush with a little mustard. Broil for about 4–5 minutes on each side until cooked through but still moist and juicy.

Drain the potatoes. Gently heat the cream and garlic in a frying pan, and then stir in the potatoes and chives; season to taste. Spoon onto serving plates and top with broiled pork chops; serve with the beet chutney.

NUTRITION NOTES PER SERVING: calories 679 | protein 27.9 g | carbohydrate 36.2 g fat 47.9 g | saturated fat 24.27 g | fiber 3 g | added sugar 2.6 g | salt 0.84 g

chile-jam ham steaks

You can't beat the taste of a juicy ham steak, and it's especially delicious with my sweet chile-jam sauce and crispy corn fritters. You can use a can of creamed corn instead, but add one less egg and no milk.

SERVES 2 | **PREPARATION: 10 MINS | COOKING TIME: 20 MINS**

2 x 6 oz (175 g) smoked
  ham steaks
1–2 tablespoons sunflower oil
1 onion, finely chopped
2 garlic cloves, finely chopped
2 red chiles, seeded and
  finely chopped
juice of 1 orange
1 tablespoon clear honey
1 tablespoon malt vinegar
2 tablespoons tomato ketchup

FOR THE FRITTERS
2 eggs
4 tablespoons milk
½ cup self-rising flour
¼ cup cornstarch
1 x 10 oz (275 g) can
  corn, drained
vegetable oil for frying
salt and pepper

Brush the ham steaks with a little oil and cook under a hot broiler or in a frying pan for 3–4 minutes on each side until cooked through.

Meanwhile, make the jam: heat the remaining oil in a small pan, add the onion, and cook for 2–3 minutes. Add the garlic and chiles, and cook for another 2 minutes until softened. Stir in the orange juice, honey, vinegar, and tomato ketchup, and simmer gently for 5 minutes.

To make the corn fritters, crack the eggs into a large bowl and whisk in the milk, flour, and cornstarch to make a smooth batter. Stir in the corn and plenty of seasoning. Cook large spoonfuls of the corn mixture in a hot, oiled frying pan for 3–4 minutes on each side until crisp and golden; repeat to make six pancakes.

Place the ham and corn fritters on a plate, spoon over a little dollop of the chile jam and serve.

NUTRITION NOTES PER SERVING: calories 963 | protein 66.6 g | carbohydrate 75.1 g fat 46.1 g | saturated fat 12.59 g | fiber 3.6 g | added sugar 18.3 g | salt 12.37 g

MEAT

french-style pork with root purée

Ooh la-la! This *chic* supper has plenty of French flair and presents beautifully. Unlike any other recipe in this book, however, this dish does need a little forward planning, as the prunes need soaking in advance to suck up the wine for plumpness and flavor.

SERVES 2 | PREPARATION: 10 MINS | COOKING TIME: 15 MINS

FOR THE MASH
8 oz (225 g) parsnips, cubed
8 oz (225 g) floury potatoes, cubed
3–4 tablespoons milk
3 tablespoons butter
salt and freshly ground pepper

FOR THE PORK
8 oz (225 g) tenderloin pork fillet, cut into ½ inch (1 cm) slices

1 tablespoon flour, seasoned with salt and pepper
¼ cup butter
8 ready-to-eat prunes soaked for at least 30 mins in ⅔ cup dry white wine
1 tablespoon redcurrant or cranberry jelly
⅔ cup heavy cream
juice of ½ lemon
salt and pepper

Cook the parsnips and potatoes in a large pan of boiling, salted water for 10–12 minutes until tender. Dust the pork with the seasoned flour, shaking off any excess. Heat half the butter in a large frying pan and, when foaming, cook the pork for 1–2 minutes on each side. Remove and set aside.

Strain the wine into the hot pan and bring to a boil. Stir in the redcurrant jelly and cook for another 2 minutes, stirring until melted. Add the cream, prunes, and pork, season to taste, and simmer gently for 2–3 minutes until the pork is cooked through.

Drain the root vegetables and mash well. Add the milk and remaining butter, and whizz with an electric hand whisk until smooth and puréed; season to taste.

Squeeze a little lemon juice into the pork pan and check the seasoning. Pile the mash onto serving plates and spoon over the pork mixture.

NUTRITION NOTES PER SERVING: calories 1149 | protein 32 g | carbohydrate 63.5 g fat 83.4 g | saturated fat 49.47 g | fiber 9.2 g | added sugar 5.2 g | salt 1.89 g

The prunes can be soaked for up to 8 hours, so pop them into the wine before you go to work, and they'll be ready when you get home.

MEAT

pasta cream bean dream

A rhyming seasonal spaghetti dish that is poetry on the plate.

11 oz (300 g) spaghetti
11 oz (300 g) green beans, sliced on the diagonal
1 tablespoon olive oil
1 onion, sliced
6 slices bacon, cut into strips
1 cup half-fat crème fraîche
3 tablespoons vegetable stock
1 lettuce, finely shredded
salt and pepper
freshly grated Parmesan, to serve

Cook the spaghetti in a large pan of boiling, salted water, according to the package directions, adding the runner beans for the last 4 minutes of cooking time.

Meanwhile, heat the oil in a frying pan and cook the onion and bacon for 5 minutes until nicely browned. Stir in the crème fraîche and stock, and simmer gently for 1 minute, without boiling.

Drain the spaghetti and beans, and return to the pan. Stir in the crème fraîche sauce and shredded lettuce, and season to taste. Transfer to serving plates and sprinkle with Parmesan and plenty of freshly ground black pepper.

NUTRITION NOTES PER SERVING: calories 496 | protein 20 g | carbohydrate 64 g fat 20 g | saturated fat 7 g | fiber 4 g | added sugar none | salt 1.77 g

You can use another type of pasta, such as tagliatelle or linguine, instead of spaghetti.

marvelous chile-cheese meatballs

My meatballs are marvelous! Well, so the wife keeps telling me. What do you think? I've made them with pork, but any lean ground meat will do just as well. You could also serve the meatballs with other types of pasta, like linguine, spaghettini, tagliatelle, taglioni, or fettucine, to name but a few.

SERVES 2 **PREPARATION: 10 MINS | COOKING TIME: 20 MINS**

8 oz lean ground pork
4 green onions, finely chopped
2 garlic cloves, finely chopped
1 red chile, seeded and
   finely chopped
2 tablespoons freshly grated
   Parmesan, plus extra to serve
2 teaspoons fresh thyme leaves

1 tablespoon olive oil
scant ½ cup red wine
5 oz (150 g) spaghetti or tagliatelle
1 x 14 oz (400 g) can chopped
tomatoes
1 dried bay leaf
pinch of sugar
salt and pepper

Mix together the pork, green onions, garlic, chile, Parmesan, thyme, and plenty of salt and pepper. Shape into 12 small, firm balls. Heat the oil in a large pan and cook the meatballs for 3–4 minutes, shaking the pan frequently, until well browned. Pour in the red wine and bubble vigorously for 1–2 minutes.

Cook the pasta in a large pan of boiling, salted water according to package directions. Stir the chopped tomatoes, bay leaf, sugar, and salt and pepper into the meatballs; bring to a boil and simmer for 8–10 minutes until the meatballs are cooked through.

Drain the pasta and return to the pan; spoon in some of the tomato sauce and toss well together. Transfer to large serving bowls and spoon over the chile-cheese meatballs with the sauce; sprinkle liberally with Parmesan and serve.

NUTRITION NOTES PER SERVING: calories 587 | protein 38.3 g | carbohydrate 64.4 g fat 17.7 g | saturated fat 5.42 g | fiber 4 g | added sugar 0.5 g | salt 0.89

pavarotti pasta

I'm sure you've heard of the three tenors; well, this is the three cheeses – and when you taste this dish, you'll be singing their praises. "Nice aroma, nice aroma." Well, what can you find that rhymes with *"Nessun dorma"*?

SERVES 4 | PREPARATION: 5 MINS | COOKING TIME: 15 MINS

12 oz (350 g) pasta shapes, such as penne or fusilli
6 slices rindless bacon, chopped
4 oz (100 g) Mozzarella, finely chopped
¾ cup grated Cheddar
½ cup grated Parmesan
⅔ cup light cream
2–3 tablespoons milk (optional)
salt and pepper
green salad leaves, to serve

Cook the pasta in a pan of boiling salted water for about **12** minutes, according to the package directions.

Meanwhile, heat a small frying pan; then cook the bacon until crispy. Drain on paper towels.

Drain the pasta and return it to the pan. Stir in the Mozzarella, Cheddar, Parmesan, and cream, and cook over a low heat, stirring, for **1–2** minutes, until the sauce is just warmed through. If the sauce is too thick, thin it by adding a little milk. Season with salt and pepper to taste.

Arrange the salad leaves on four serving plates. Spoon the pasta in creamy sauce on top, and serve sprinkled with the crispy bacon bits. Wash down with a bottle of Cava.

NUTRITION NOTES PER SERVING: calories 772 | protein 34 g | carbohydrate 68 g
fat 42 g | saturated fat 22 g | fiber 3 g | added sugar none | salt 3.09 g

my maddie's spicy sausages

My kids and I love to shape up these sausage treats and like to eat them with spicy potato wedges and a tasty smoky sauce.

SERVES 4 | **PREPARATION: 15 MINS | COOKING TIME: 15 MINS**

FOR THE PATTIES

1 lb (450 g) herby sausages
4 green onions, finely chopped
1 tablespoon cranberry sauce
2 tablespoons flour, seasoned with
   salt and pepper
1 tablespoon sunflower oil

FOR THE POTATO WEDGES

4 x 7 oz (200 g) baking potatoes,
   cooked and cooled
1–2 tablespoons olive oil

¼ teaspoon salt
¼ teaspoon ground cumin
a pinch of cayenne

SMOKY SAUCE

juice of 1 orange
1 tablespoon clear honey
1 tablespoon malt vinegar
2 tablespoons tomato ketchup
1 tablespoon dark soy sauce
1 teaspoon English mustard

To make the patties, skin the sausages and mix with the green onions, cranberry sauce, and plenty of seasoning. Shape the mixture into eight sausage shapes; then dust with the seasoned flour. Heat the sunflower oil in a large frying pan and cook the patties for 5–6 minutes on each side until well browned and cooked through.

Make the potato wedges: cut each potato into eight wedges and brush with the olive oil. Stir together the salt, cumin, and cayenne, and sprinkle over the wedges. Brush a griddle pan or large frying pan with a little more oil and cook the wedges for 3–4 minutes on each side until crisp and golden.

Meanwhile, make the smoky sauce: in a small pan heat together the orange juice, honey, vinegar, ketchup, soy sauce, and mustard; bring to a boil and simmer rapidly for 2–3 minutes until slightly thickened. Arrange the patties and potato wedges on serving plates and spoon over a dollop of the smoky sauce. Great with some nice fresh lemonade. Yes please, Dad!

NUTRITION NOTES PER SERVING: calories 689 | protein 17.3 g | carbohydrate 63.8 g fat 42.2 g | saturated fat 14.65 g | fiber 3.5 g | added sugar 8.4 g | salt 3.36 g

This dish is great served with crispy onion rings. Simply slice a large onion into rings and soak in a little milk for 10–15 minutes. Drain well, dust with seasoned flour, and deep-fry until crisp and golden – delicious!

double-quick caroline's cassoulet

Cassoulet, like paella, can be made in many different styles. Goose or duck confits and sausages with bacon or salt pork or lamb are all delicious. It can take up to three days to prepare, but here is my own double-quick version. It's my producer, Caroline's, favorite nibble.

SERVES 4 | **PREPARATION: 10 MINS | COOKING TIME: 40 MINS**

1 tablespoon olive oil
1 onion, chopped
2 garlic cloves, finely chopped
9 oz (250 g) each cubed lamb or pork
6 slices smoked bacon, roughly chopped
1 x 14 oz (400 g) can tomatoes
2 carrots, diced
⅔ cup red wine
⅔ cup lamb stock
1 teaspoon each fresh, or ¼ teaspoon each dried, rosemary, thyme, and parsley
1 x 14 oz (400 g) can haricot beans, drained
2 tablespoons fresh white breadcrumbs
salt and pepper
chopped fresh parsley, to garnish

Heat the oil in a large pan and cook the onion and garlic for 3–4 minutes until softened. Add the lamb or pork and bacon and stir-fry for 5 minutes.

Stir in the tomatoes, carrots, wine, stock, and herbs; then cover and cook over a medium heat for 20–25 minutes until the meat is tender.

Preheat the broiler to high. Stir the beans into the pan, season with salt and pepper, and transfer to a heatproof serving dish. Sprinkle over the breadcrumbs; then broil for a few minutes until the topping is golden. Sprinkle with the chopped parsley and serve with a nice fresh red wine.

NUTRITION NOTES PER SERVING: calories 520 | protein 38 g | carbohydrate 23 g
fat 28 g | saturated fat 11 g | fiber 6 g | added sugar none | salt 2.3 g

MEAT

156

mustard basil beef rolls

Beef and mustard is a fantastic combination; this dish also tastes great using that other classic accompaniment, creamed horseradish, in place of the mustard.

SERVES 2 | **PREPARATION: 10 MINS | COOKING TIME: 15 MINS**

2 x 6 oz (175 g) sirloin steaks, trimmed
1 tablespoon English mustard
2 garlic cloves, crushed
4 tablespoons chopped fresh basil or parsley
1 teaspoon cracked black peppercorns
2 tablespoons butter, at room temperature
1 tablespoon olive oil
1 small onion, finely chopped
2 tablespoons brandy
⅔ cup heavy cream
a pinch of superfine sugar
salt and pepper
steamed new potatoes or mash and steamed, buttered cabbage, to serve

Place the steaks on a sheet of plastic wrap and cover with another sheet. Bat out with a rolling pin until ¼ inch (6 mm) thick. Remove the plastic wrap. Mix together the mustard, garlic, half the basil or parsley, peppercorns, and butter until well blended. Spread the mixture onto the steaks, roll up tightly, and secure with string or wooden toothpicks.

Heat the oil in a frying pan and cook the steaks for 6–8 minutes, turning frequently until well browned. Remove the steaks from the pan, cover and rest for 3–4 minutes. Add the onion to the steak pan and cook for 2 minutes until beginning to soften. Stir in the brandy and bubble vigorously for 1 minute. Stir in the cream and heat through for 1–2 minutes. Season with salt, pepper, and superfine sugar to taste, and stir in the remaining basil or parsley.

Remove the string or toothpicks and serve the beef roulades with your choice of potatoes, buttered cabbage, and creamy basil sauce.

NUTRITION NOTES PER SERVING: calories 877 | protein 33.3 g | carbohydrate 9.9 g
fat 74.7 g | saturated fat 39.65 g | fiber 0.7 g | added sugar 0.5 g | salt 1.35 g

MEAT

beefburgers with blue cheese sauce

I always find a tasty beefburger a hard thing to turn down. And these are really easy to make and have a lovely, juicy texture . . . yum!

SERVES 2	PREPARATION: 10 MINS	COOKING TIME: 10 MINS

9 oz (250 g) lean ground beef
4 small pickles, finely chopped
3 tablespoons chopped fresh parsley
1 egg yolk
1 tablespoon sunflower oil
1 tablespoon Dijon mustard
2 tablespoons mayonnaise
2 oz (50 g) blue cheese such as Stilton or Gorgonzola, crumbled
salt and pepper
seeded burger buns, shredded lettuce, and sliced tomato, to serve

---

Mix together the ground beef, pickles, parsley, egg yolk, and plenty of salt and pepper. Shape the mixture into even-size burgers.

Brush the burgers with a little oil and cook in a hot frying pan for 3–4 minutes on each side until well browned but still a little pink in the center.

Meanwhile, stir together the mustard and mayonnaise; then gently fold in the blue cheese.

Serve the burgers in seeded buns with plenty of salad and a good dollop of the blue cheese dressing.

NUTRITION NOTES PER SERVING: calories 516 | protein 34 g | carbohydrate 1.6 g
fat 41.6 g | saturated fat 11.83 g | fiber 0.9 g | added sugar none | salt 1.74 g

peppered nugget steak

I cook this dish time and again when I'm entertaining – it makes a lovely dinner-party main course.

SERVES 2 | **PREPARATION: 15 MINS | COOKING TIME: 15 MINS**

2 x 5 oz (150 g) beef tournedos
2 tablespoons cracked black
  peppercorns
1 tablespoon olive oil
4 oz (100 g) chestnut mushrooms,
  thinly sliced
2 tablespoons brandy
⅔ cup red wine
1 teaspoon fresh thyme leaves or
  ¼ teaspoon dried thyme
1 tablespoon redcurrant or
  cranberry jelly

1 teaspoon balsamic or
  sherry vinegar
salt and pepper

FOR THE POTATO GALETTES
8 oz (225 g) potato, coarsely grated
2 tablespoons all-purpose flour
1 tablespoon olive oil
small fresh thyme sprig or
  whole chives, to garnish

Place the steak on a board and sprinkle generously with the cracked peppercorns, pressing them into the surface of the steak with your fingertips. Brush the steaks with the oil and sprinkle with a little salt. Cook the steaks in a hot frying pan for 3–4 minutes on each side until well browned but still a little pink in the center. Meanwhile, make the potato galettes: mix together the potato, flour, and a little salt. Heat the oil in a separate frying pan and, dividing the potato mixture into two, drop in two small piles of potato; flatten down with a fish slice, and cook for 3–4 minutes on each side until crisp and golden. Remove the steaks from the pan, place on a plate, and cover to keep warm. Add the mushrooms to the steak pan and stir-fry for a minute or so until beginning to brown. Pour the brandy into the hot pan and carefully ignite. When the flames have died down, stir in the wine, thyme, redcurrant jelly, and vinegar, and boil for 2–3 minutes, stirring until the jelly dissolves; season to taste. Place the potato galettes on two serving plates and top with the steaks. Spoon around the mushroom sauce, garnish with herbs, and serve.

NUTRITION NOTES PER SERVING: calories 597 | protein 37.5 g | carbohydrate 51 g fat 19.2 g | saturated fat 4.45 g | fiber 2.6 g | added sugar 5.2 g | salt 0.3 g

If you don't have a mortar and pestle, place whole black peppercorns in a small, strong plastic bag and bash with a heavy rolling pin.

MEAT

it's time to over indulge

desserts

164	MERRY BERRY CHRISTMAS CRUMBLE	50 MINS
167	GOLDEN SUNGLAZED APRICOT RICE	30 MINS
168	LEMON CARAMEL STRAWBERRY NESTS	25 MINS
171	SYDNEY'S FRUIT COCONUT SMOOTHIE	15 MINS
172	CHOCOLATE-ORANGE DRIZZLE FRUIT	30 MINS
174	SCRUNCHED SPICED APPLE CREAM PIE	20 MINS
175	AMAZING MANGO MARZIPAN TARTLETS	25 MINS
177	MANGO CRANBERRY NUT CRUMBLE	45 MINS
178	TERRIFIC TOFFEE-CHOC CAKE DESSERT	20 MINS
179	ZAPPED LEMON CURD DESSERT	11 MINS
180	CARAMEL ALASKAS	20 MINS
183	CRACKINGLY FRUITY MOUNT VESUVIUS	20 MINS
184	CHOCO-NANA BRANDY SNAPS	10 MINS
185	CITRUS BANANA SOUFFLÉ OMELET	15 MINS
186	TITILLATING TARTY RHUBY SOUFLETTE	20 MINS
189	SILVANA'S ORANGE TAGLIATELLE SUZETTE	25 MINS

merry berry christmas crumble

This is my idea of a treat for any day of the week – and it's a great way to use up the left-over mincemeat and cranberries that have been hanging around since Christmas!

SERVES 4   PREPARATION: 15 MINS | COOKING TIME: 35 MINS

4 pears or eating apples, cored and sliced
⅓ cup fresh or frozen cranberries
2 tablespoons orange juice
1 banana, thickly sliced
3–4 tablespoons mincemeat
¼ cup butter, cut into pieces
4 oz (100 g) all-purpose flour
2 tablespoons light raw brown sugar
custard, to serve

Preheat the oven to 375°F (190°C). Place the pear or apple slices, cranberries, and orange juice in a pan, cover and cook over a low heat for 7–8 minutes until the fruit is beginning to soften. Remove from the heat and stir in the banana and mincemeat; then transfer to a pie dish.

Rub the butter into the flour until it resembles fine breadcrumbs; then stir in the sugar. Spoon over the fruit and bake for 20–25 minutes until the topping is golden. Serve immediately with custard.

NUTRITION NOTES PER SERVING: calories 357 | protein 3.5 g | carbohydrate 63.1 g
fat 11.8 g | saturated fat 7.15 g | fiber 5.3 g | added sugar 9.7 g | salt 0.33 g

golden sunglazed apricot rice

Flaked rice makes this dessert incredibly quick, as it's so easy to use, and the finished dish is simply gorgeous. For an extra richness, add four tablespoons of cream to the rice while cooking.

SERVES 4 | **PREPARATION: 10 MINS | COOKING TIME: 20 MINS**

¼ cup ready-to-eat dried apricots
⅓ cup golden raisins
1 lemon
½ cup flaked rice
3¼ cups semiskim milk
¼ cup superfine sugar
8 tablespoons apricot jam
fresh mint sprigs, to decorate

Reserve 4 of the dried apricots; then chop the rest. Mix together the chopped dried apricots and raisins, and set aside. Using a swivel-style vegetable peeler, cut wide strips of rind from the lemon.

Place the lemon-rind strips, rice, milk, and sugar in a pan and bring to a boil; then reduce the heat and simmer for 12–15 minutes, stirring often. Stir in the dried fruit, divide between four serving bowls, and set aside to cool slightly.

To make the apricot glaze, squeeze 1 tablespoon of juice from the lemon into a small pan. Stir in 2 tablespoons of water; then add the jam. Bring to a boil, stirring, until the jam has melted; then immediately remove from the heat. Leave for a few minutes to cool and thicken slightly; then pour over the rice puddings. Decorate each with a dried apricot and a mint sprig.

NUTRITION NOTES PER SERVING: calories 373 | protein 9 g | carbohydrate 82 g
fat 3 g | saturated fat 2 g | fiber 2 g | added sugar 41 g | salt 0.27 g

lemon caramel strawberry nests

If you like the taste of toffee apples, just wait until you taste these sticky summer desserts that are literally assembled in minutes. Go on, get tacky!

SERVES 4 | PREPARATION: 15 MINS | COOKING TIME: 10 MINS

9 oz (200 g) Mascarpone cheese
⅔ cup light cream
1 tablespoon confectioners' sugar
9 oz (200 g) strawberries, hulled
4 ready-made meringue nests
3 oz (75 g) superfine sugar
3 tablespoons fresh lemon juice
2 tablespoons chopped toasted hazelnuts

Beat together the Mascarpone cheese, cream, and confectioners' sugar until smooth. Reserve four of the strawberries and chop the remainder. Stir the chopped strawberries into the cream mixture and use to fill the meringue baskets. Slice the reserved strawberries and stick the slices into the cream. Place each in the center of a serving plate.

Gently heat the superfine sugar and lemon juice in a heavy-bottomed pan, set over a very low heat, stirring until the sugar dissolves. Increase the heat and let the mixture bubble for about 4 minutes until golden – as the mixture cooks, don't stir, but swirl the pan occasionally so it doesn't burn around the edges.

Remove from the heat and add the chopped hazelnuts and a tablespoon of water. Swirl to combine; then immediately pour over the meringue nests and serve.

NUTRITION NOTES PER SERVING: calories 681 | protein 7 g | carbohydrate 76 g
fat 41 g | saturated fat 23 g | fiber 1 g | added sugar 67 g | salt 0.34 g

sydney's fruit coconut smoothie

A fruit smoothie is a refreshingly delicious Australian-style summer drink, but it also doubles up well as a silky sauce for these cool fruity puddings.

SERVES 4   **PREPARATION: 15 MINS**

12 oz (350 g) strawberries, halved or sliced
2 nectarines or peaches, stoned and sliced
4 oz (100 g) blueberries or black grapes
1 large banana
½ cup fresh orange juice
scant 1 cup Greek yogurt
2 tablespoons dried coconut, toasted

Mix together the strawberries, nectarines or peaches, and blueberries or grapes and divide between four tall glass dessert dishes.

To make the fruit smoothie, roughly chop the banana; then place in a food processor or blender with the orange juice and yogurt and process until smooth.

Pour the smoothie over the fruit in the bowls and sprinkle each with toasted dried coconut; serve.

NUTRITION NOTES PER SERVING: calories 201 | protein 6 g | carbohydrate 26 g
fat 9 g | saturated fat 6 g | fiber 4 g | added sugar none | salt 0.11 g

For a really cool smoothie, peel the banana, cover in plastic wrap and place in the freezer for 1–2 hours. Cut the banana in half, place in a food processor or blender with the orange juice and yogurt, and process until smooth.

chocolate-orange drizzle fruit

This fruity concoction cries out for a rich drizzle of chocolate, so how could I resist? It's a fantastic finale to any meal.

SERVES 4	PREPARATION: 15 MINS	COOKING TIME: 15 MINS

2 oranges
4 tablespoons butter
4 tablespoons light raw brown sugar
2 tablespoons fresh lemon juice
2 pears, peeled, halved, and cored
2 apples, peeled, quartered, and cored
3 oz (75 g) plain chocolate, broken into pieces
4 tablespoons whipping or heavy cream

Using a zester, remove the rind from one orange and set aside. Finely grate 1 teaspoon of rind from the second orange and reserve. Using a sharp knife, remove and discard the remaining rind and pith from both oranges, reserving any juices. Slice the fruit thickly.

Melt the butter in a frying pan and add the sugar and stir until dissolved. Stir in the rind from the first orange, the lemon juice, orange slices, pears, and apples, and cook for 5 minutes until softened.

Microwave the chocolate on high for 1½–2 minutes (or set the bowl over a pan of simmering water) until melted. Stir in the teaspoon of orange rind, reserved orange juice and cream.

Divide the fruit between serving bowls, spoon over the juices, and drizzle over the chocolate sauce.

NUTRITION NOTES PER SERVING: calories 459 | protein 3 g | carbohydrate 53 g fat 28 g | saturated fat 17 g | fibre 4 g | added sugar 32 g | salt 0.3 g

DESSERTS

scrunched spiced apple cream pie

Forget boring old apple tarts, this spiced-up pie has a brandy-cream layer and a scrunchy, crunchy phyllo-topping . . . delicious!

SERVES 2 | PREPARATION: 10 MINS | COOKING TIME: 10 MINS

FOR THE FILLING
4 tablespoons butter
2¼ lb (1 kg) Cortland or Rome
   Beauty apples,
peeled, cored and sliced
2 oz (50 g) superfine sugar
½ teaspoon ground cinnamon
½ teaspoon ground ginger

FOR THE TOPPING
6 sheets phyllo pastry
2 tablespoons melted butter
confectioners' sugar, for dusting
4 tablespoons brandy
1 tablespoon light
   raw brown sugar

Preheat the oven to 425°F (220°C).

Heat the butter in a large pan and throw in the apple slices. Sprinkle over the sugar, cinnamon, and ginger, and cook for 3 minutes, stirring frequently. Cover and cook gently for another 5 minutes until softened.

Meanwhile, brush the phyllo sheets with the melted butter and roughly scrunch up. Place on a baking sheet and dust with confectioners' sugar. Bake for 6–7 minutes until golden brown.

Spoon the apple mixture into a buttered pie dish; keep warm. Swirl the brandy into the pan; then stir in the light raw brown sugar and cream, and cook for 2–3 minutes, scraping up any residue on the bottom of the pan with a wooden spoon.

Pour the cream sauce over the apple mixture; then arrange the scrunched phyllo on top. Dust with a little extra icing sugar and serve warm.

NUTRITION NOTES PER SERVING: calories 1202 | protein 7 g | carbohydrate 129.7 g
fat 69 g | saturated fat 42.47 g | fiber 7.6 g | added sugar 40.8 g | salt 2.17 g

amazing mango marzipan tartlets

So . . . how do you like your tarts? Oooh, perhaps with plums, or you might prefer apricots. But for me it has to be a nice ripe mango. Believe me, once bitten, forever smitten!

SERVES 4   PREPARATION: 10 MINS | COOKING TIME: 15 MINS

9 oz (250 g) puff pastry
5 oz (150 g) marzipan, cut into 4 x ¼ inch (6 mm) thick slices
2 mangoes
4 tablespoons lemon curd
⅔ cup heavy cream, whipped to soft peaks

Preheat the oven to 425°F (220°C).

Roll the puff pastry on a lightly floured surface to make an 11 inch (28 cm) square. Cut into four equal-sized squares and transfer to a baking sheet. Cut each marzipan slice into two triangles. Place two of the triangles, overlapping slightly, in the center of each pastry square.

Slice each mango down both sides of its central pit. Peel, then make lengthwise cuts through each piece of mango, almost to the end. Gently press down on the mango to fan out the slices.

Place one mango fan, flat-side down, on the center of each pastry square; then spread 1 tablespoon of lemon curd over each piece of mango. Bake for 12–15 minutes until the pastry is risen and golden.

Meanwhile, remove any remaining flesh from around the mango pits and chop finely; stir into the whipped cream. Serve the tarts warm with a dollop of the mango cream.

NUTRITION NOTES PER SERVING: calories 638 | protein 6.8 g | carbohydrate 69.5 g fat 39 g | saturated fat 11.72 g | fiber 2.7 g | added sugar 24.5 g | salt 0.57 g

mango cranberry nut crumble

I don't know anyone who can resist the tempting taste of a mouthwatering crumble, so here's one that keeps that tradition going. Canned mango is a great pantry standby. Its sweet and juicy flesh works brilliantly in this tropical nut crumble.

SERVES 4 | PREPARATION: 10 MINS | COOKING TIME: 35 MINS

¼ cup dried or ready-to-eat cranberries
grated rind and juice of 1 large orange
1¼ cups all-purpose flour
½ cup butter, chilled and diced
⅓ cup superfine sugar
¼ cup slivered almonds, roughly chopped
½ teaspoon ground mixed spice
1 x 14 oz (400 g) can mango slices in syrup, drained
custard or cream, to serve

Preheat the oven to 375°F (190°C).

Place the cranberries and orange juice in a small pan and gently bring to a boil; remove from the heat and set aside for 5 minutes.

Meanwhile, place the flour and butter in a large bowl; then, using the fingertips, rub together until the mixture resembles coarse breadcrumbs. Stir in the superfine sugar, almonds, and mixed spice.

Stir together the cranberries and orange juice, and mix with the mango slices and the orange rind. Spoon the mixture into a buttered pie dish and sprinkle over the crumble. Bake in the oven for 25–30 minutes until golden brown. Serve with hot custard or pouring cream.

NUTRITION NOTES PER SERVING: calories 498 | protein 5.4 g | carbohydrate 68.5 g fat 24.4 g | saturated fat 13.35 g | fiber 2.2 g | added sugar 27.2 g | salt 0.49 g

terrific toffee-choc cake dessert

Once again it's time to overindulge – that's if you consider a dessert like this a naughty treat. It's simply heavenly and delicious, so just slap it on those thighs, as me wife would say.

SERVES 4   PREPARATION: 10 MINS | COOKING TIME: 10 MINS

a 6 oz (175 g) block ready-made chocolate or marble cake
2 tablespoons brandy (optional)
¼ cup butter, plus extra for melting
⅔ cup light raw brown sugar
3 tablespoons light corn syrup
⅔ cup heavy cream
¼ cup toasted hazelnuts, chopped
1 banana, sliced
rind and juice of 1 small orange
confectioners' sugar and fresh mint sprigs, to decorate

Preheat the oven to 400°F (200°C).

Cut the cake into ½ inch (1 cm) thick slices. Place in a small, shallow ovenproof dish and drizzle over the brandy, if using.

Place ¼ cup of the butter in a small pan with the sugar and light corn syrup. Stir over a low heat until the butter is melted and the sugar dissolved. Stir in the cream and remove from the heat. Pour the sauce over the cake and sprinkle with the nuts. Bake for 10 minutes until the sauce is bubbling.

Meanwhile, heat a small knob of butter in a small frying pan. Add the banana slices and orange rind, and cook briefly until golden. Pour in the orange juice and remove from the heat.

Place a slice of cake on each serving plate. Spoon over some sauce, top with banana slices, dust with confectioners' sugar, and decorate each with a mint sprig.

NUTRITION NOTES PER SERVING: calories 688 | protein 5 g | carbohydrate 69 g
fat 44 g | saturated fat 25 g | fiber 1 g | added sugar 51 g | salt 0.9 g

zapped lemon curd dessert

The microwave is an amazing way to cook light and fluffy desserts in no time at all. This tangy lemon dessert can be served with hot custard or whipped cinnamon-flavored cream.

SERVES 4   PREPARATION: 5 MINS | COOKING TIME: 6 MINS

½ cup butter
½ cup superfine sugar
1 cup self-rising flour
2 eggs, beaten
grated rind of 1 lemon
4 tablespoons lemon curd
custard or whipped cinnamon-flavored cream, to serve
fresh mint springs, to decorate

Place the butter, sugar, flour, eggs, and lemon rind in a food processor and whizz together until well blended.

Drop a tablespoon of lemon curd into the bottom of four buttered, heatproof teacups. Spoon the batter mixture on top; cover with microfilm and microwave individually on high for 1½ minutes until risen and cooked through. Rest for 1 minute before serving.

Pour the custard on top of each sponge and serve in the cup, or turn out onto small plates and pour the custard around the bottom of each. Alternatively, whip some cream with a pinch of cinnamon and put a dollop on top of each dessert. Spike with a mint sprig and serve.

NUTRITION NOTES PER SERVING: calories 444 | protein 5.6 g | carbohydrate 54.6 g
fat 24.2 g | saturated fat 13.8 g | fiber 0.8 g | added sugar 32.3 g | salt 0.82 g

caramel
alaskas

This glamorous dessert is my own up-market version of the classic baked Alaska, with the light raw brown sugar in the meringue adding a delicious caramel flavor. At Christmas time, why not try replacing the Madeira cake with Christmas cake?

SERVES 4　　PREPARATION: 15 MINS | COOKING TIME: 5 MINS

3-4 tablespoons ground almonds
4 scoops raspberry ripple or vanilla ice cream
4 x ½ inch (1 cm) thick square Madeira cake slices
2-3 tablespoons brandy
9-12 mandarin segments
3 egg whites
1¼ cups light raw brown sugar
confectioners' sugar, for dusting

Place the ground almonds on a plate and roll the ice cream scoops in them. Place on a baking sheet and open-freeze for 30 minutes until firm.

Place the cake slices well apart on a baking sheet. Drizzle with brandy and arrange the mandarin segments end-to-end to make a ring in the center of each slice. Place an almond-covered ice-cream scoop in the middle of each ring. Return to the freezer while you make the meringue.

Preheat the oven to 450°F (230°C). Place the egg whites in a clean, grease-free bowl. Whisk in the sugar, a tablespoon at a time, whisking thoroughly after each addition until the mixture forms soft peaks. Spoon the meringue over the ice cream and spread to cover. Bake for about 5 minutes until the meringue starts to brown. Transfer to the serving plates, dust with confectioners' sugar, and serve immediately.

NUTRITION NOTES PER SERVING: calories 477 | protein 8.6 g | carbohydrate 73.7 g fat 16.6 g | saturated fat 5.65 g | fiber 1.4 g | added sugar 62.4 g | salt 0.41 g

crackingly fruity mount vesuvius

What a spectacular dessert! Eat this and the earth really will move!

SERVES 4 | PREPARATION: 15 MINS | COOKING TIME: 5 MINS

9 oz (250 g) mixed fruit such as strawberries, mango, and grapes, cut into chunks
1 tablespoon superfine sugar
2 tablespoons white rum
2 oz (50 g) amaretti or almond macaroons

FOR THE CARAMEL
½ cup superfine sugar
juice of 1 lemon

FOR THE TOPPING
9 oz (250 g) Mascarpone cheese
2 tablespoons white rum
2 tablespoons confectioners' sugar
grated rind of 1 lemon
fresh mint sprigs, to serve

Place the fruit, superfine sugar, and rum in a large bowl and mix well together; set aside for 5 minutes.

For the caramel, place the sugar, lemon juice, and a splash of water in a small pan. Heat gently, stirring until the sugar dissolves; then raise the heat and boil rapidly, without stirring, until golden.

Meanwhile, for the topping, mix together the Mascarpone, rum, confectioners' sugar, and lemon rind.

Arrange the cookies in the bottom of four individual dishes and spoon over the fruit mixture. Spoon the flavored Mascarpone on top of the fruit, shaping it to a tall peak in the center.

Pour caramel over the top of each and set aside for a minute or two until the caramel sets; then serve immediately, decorated with mint sprigs.

NUTRITION NOTES PER SERVING: calories 508 | protein 3.2 g | carbohydrate 47 g
fat 31.5 g | saturated fat 18.2 g | fiber 1.3 g | added sugar 28.9 g | salt 0.18 g

choco-nana brandy snaps

Chocolate and banana whip up with fromage frais to make a yummy filling for ready-made brandy snaps - ideal for a quick dessert. For an attractive decoration slice an unskinned banana, dust liberally with confectioners' sugar, and pop under a hot broiler until caramelized and golden.

SERVES 4 | PREPARATION: 5 MINS | COOKING TIME: 5 MINS

4 oz dark chocolate
1 large banana, roughly chopped
scant 1 cup plain yogurt
1 tablespoon confectioners' sugar, plus extra, to dust
a few drops of vanilla extract
¼ cup slivered or chopped hazelnuts, toasted
8 brandy snaps
1 extra banana, to decorate (optional)

Break the chocolate into a heatproof bowl and microwave on high for 1½–2 minutes, or sit over a pan of simmering water, stirring occasionally, until melted.

Place the banana in a food processor and whizz to make a smooth purée. Add the fromage frais, confectioners' sugar and vanilla extract and blend again, then with the motor running, slowly drizzle in the chocolate until smooth and well blended.

Stir the hazelnuts into the mixture, then spoon into a pastry bag. Pipe the filling into the brandy snaps. Dust with confectioners' sugar, decorate with banana if using, and serve.

NUTRITION NOTES PER SERVING: calories 404 | protein 6.6 g | carbohydrate 49.8 g fat 21 g | saturated fat 10.83 g | fiber 1 g | added sugar 32.4 g | salt 0.24 g

citrus banana soufflé omelet

This sweet omelet is filled with yummy banana custard – I've served my banana custard cold, but if you want to, warm it gently in a small pan. Please do remember to grate only the rind, not the white pith of the lemon, which is bitter.

SERVES 2 | **PREPARATION: 10 MINS | COOKING TIME: 5 MINS**

3 eggs, separated
1 tablespoon light raw brown sugar
a few drops of vanilla extract
2 large bananas, roughly mashed
grated rind of 1 lemon
scant ½ cup ready-made custard
a knob of butter
confectioners' sugar, to dust

Stir together the egg yolks, light raw brown sugar, and vanilla extract, and set aside. Roughly mash the bananas, add the lemon rind, and fold together with the custard.

In a large bowl whisk the egg whites until stiff; then gently fold in the egg yolk mixture. Preheat the broiler to high.

Heat the butter in an 8 inch (20 cm) frying pan and pour in the soufflé mixture. Cook for 2–3 minutes until the underside is golden; then place under a hot broiler for 1–2 minutes until puffed and golden.

Spoon the banana custard on top of the soufflé and fold in half to enclose the filling. Slide onto a plate, cut in half, and dust liberally with confectioners' sugar; serve immediately.

NUTRITION NOTES PER SERVING: calories 362 | protein 12.7 g | carbohydrate 47.3 g fat 14.8 g | saturated fat 6.41 g | fiber 1.3 g | added sugar 14 g | salt 0.47 g

If you're feeling really fancy, heat a skewer in a gas flame and press down on top of the sugar dusted soufflé – it will caramelize the sugar immediately, giving an attractive branding mark, which can be repeated to make a lattice or criss-cross effect.

DESSERTS

titillating tarty rhuby souflette

Try my puffy tarty souflette – it's packed full of spiced juicy fruit and really captures the eyes and the tastebuds.

SERVES 4	PREPARATION: 10 MINS | COOKING TIME: 10 MINS

9 oz (250 g) rhubarb, cut into 1 inch (2.5 cm) pieces
1 tablespoon orange juice or water
4 tablespoons superfine sugar
a good pinch of mixed spice
4 oz (100 g) strawberries, sliced
3 eggs, separated
1 teaspoon finely grated orange rind
a knob of butter
confectioners' sugar, for dusting
crème fraîche, to serve

Place the rhubarb, orange juice or water, 3 tablespoons of the sugar, and the mixed spice in a pan and bring to a boil; simmer for 4 minutes until tender and thickened. Stir in the strawberries and set aside.

Beat the egg yolks and remaining sugar until pale; then stir in the orange rind. In a separate bowl, whisk the egg whites until stiff. Fold the egg yolks carefully into the whites.

Preheat the broiler to medium. Melt the butter in a 9 inch (23 cm) frying pan and spoon in the egg mixture so it covers the bottom. Cook over a gentle heat for a few minutes until golden underneath and beginning to set; then broil for 1 minute until golden and puffy.

Slide the souflette onto a serving plate and spoon some of the fruit and sauce over one half. Fold over and dust liberally with confectioners' sugar. Serve in wedges with extra fruit and a dollop of crème fraîche on the side.

NUTRITION NOTES PER SERVING: calories 170 | protein 5.5 g | carbohydrate 24.6 g
fat 6.2 g | saturated fat 2.44 g | fiber 1.2 g | added sugar 22.3 g | salt 0.19 g

silvana's orange tagliatelle suzette

This version of the classic French dish Crêpes Suzette is so wonderfully satisfying and is a delightful way to finish a meal, perhaps with a glass of dessert wine.

SERVES 4 | **PREPARATION: 10 MINS | COOKING TIME: 15 MINS**

1 cup all-purpose flour
¼ teaspoon salt
1 egg, beaten
2 tablespoons melted butter
1 cup milk
sunflower oil, for frying
3 tablespoons unsalted butter
2 tablespoons superfine sugar, plus 1 teaspoon
grated rind and juice of 2 oranges
2 tablespoons brandy
cream, to serve

Sift the flour and salt into a bowl. Make a well in the center and pour in the egg, butter, and half the milk. Whisk until smooth; then gradually whisk in the remaining milk to give a smooth batter.

Heat a little oil in pancake or frying pan and swirl in 2 tablespoons of the batter; cook for a minute or so until golden, then flip and cook for 30 seconds more. Repeat to make eight pancakes. Lay the pancakes on top of each other; then roll up. Cut into wide strips.

Heat the butter in a large frying pan with the 2 tablespoons of superfine sugar and the orange juice and rind, stirring until the sugar dissolves. Toss in the pancake strips and gently heat through.

Push the pancakes to one side of the pan and increase the heat. Sprinkle the remaining teaspoon of superfine sugar onto the space in the pan and, when the sugar begins to melt and bubble, pour over the brandy; carefully ignite. Let the flames subside; then serve immediately with cream.

NUTRITION NOTES PER SERVING: calories 384 | protein 6.1 g | carbohydrate 36.5 g fat 22.9 g | saturated fat 11.12 g | fiber 0.8 g | added sugar 11.8 g | salt 0.56 g

DESSERTS

index

Italic type indicates illustrations

A

apples	164
broiled peppery pork and apple	140
cream pie, scrunched spiced	174
apricot rice, golden sunglazed	*166*, *167*
avocado salsa pasta, admired	*68*, 69

B

bacon	104
crispy batton bacon potato cakes	23
liver and bacon with tsar mash	103
bagels, flashed smoked salmon	30, *31*
bananas	171
choco-nana brandy snaps	184
citrus banana soufflé omelet	185
basil beef rolls, mustard	158
beans	
beanburgers, spicy	*58*, 59
chile bean ranch pasties, Clare's	*20*, *21*
kidney	62
lima bean purée	97
pasta cream bean dream	148, *149*
beansprout shrimp noodle, tossed	*78*, *79*
beef	
beefburgers with blue cheese sauce	159
canton stir-fried beef with noodles	141
mustard basil beef rolls	158
peppered nugget steak	*160*, 161
beetroot chutney	144
brandy snaps, choco-nana	184
bread	
eggy	29
naan	60, 111, 117
pita	36, 131
sauce	104
bream	88
broccoli, stir-fried	104
butter	
garlic	90
peanut	117

C

cabbage	126
capers	92
caramel Alaskas	180, *181*
carrots	55, 56
caserecce	53
cassoulet, double-quick Caroline's	156, *157*
cheese	
blue cheese sauce	159
bubbling webbed-cheese pasta	52
Cheddar	53, 62, 97, 152
cheese 'n' onion tarte tatin	*44*, 45
Edam	27
feta	22
Gorgonzola	159
Gruyère	29, 53, 97
marvelous chile-cheese	
meatballs	*150*, 151
Mascarpone	168, 183
Mozzarella	27, 29, 52, 98, 152
Parmesan	18, 152
Red Leicester	64
spinach and blue cheese tart	46, *47*
Stilton	46, 159
cheesecake, mighty Mexican tortilla	*62*, *63*
chicken	
Acapulco	*106*, 107
and corn soup	*16*, 17
chicken liver	103
chow mein, Chester's chicken	118, *119*
clever cook's roast	
chicken dinner	104, *105*
coq au vin, lightning	100, *101*
doodle spinach 'n' chicken	
noodle	*112*, 113
finger-licking chicken wings	*34*, 35
flash chicken satay	*116*, 117
ginger chicken with	
coconut rice	114, *115*
gorgeous chicken korma	111
honeyed tarragon quick	
chick salad	*38*, *39*
Jimmy's chicken kiev	*96*, 97
Mozzarella-oozing rosemary chicken	98
sos butter chicken with pilau rice	110
zesty chick fric	102
chile	53, 107
chile-jam ham steaks	145
chile-lemon-splashed fish	86, *87*
Clare's chile bean ranch pasties	*20*, *21*
corta spini-chile pasta	53
marvellous chile-cheese	
meatballs	*150*, 151
sauce	70
chimichangas, cha-cha-cha	108, *109*
chocolate	
choco-nana brandy snaps	184
orange drizzle fruit	172, *173*
terrific toffee-choc cake dessert	178
clam chowder with Parmesan croutons	18
cod	18, 71, 75, 86
Cawley's classic fish and chips	*92*, *93*
citrus-crusted cod with cajun spuds	88
crunch lunch cod and mash	*84*, 85
kebabs with Aztec salsa	*82*, *83*
rocky road potato cod	89
coley	75
corn	
and chicken soup	*16*, 17
fritters	145
couscous	56, 86
crabmeat	69
cracklingly fruity Mount Vesuvius	*182*, 183
cranberries	164
mango cranberry nut crumble	*176*, 177
crêpes, spiked green onion supper	*32*, 33
croutons	18, 71
crumbles	
mango cranberry nut	*176*, 177
merry berry Christmas	164, *165*
curry, wan kai Thai-style red	75

D

duck, Peking	*124*, 125
duckling, succulent spiced	*126*, *127*
dumplings with spicy broth, turkey	99

E

eggplant supper stacks, Ainsley's	*24*, 25
eggs	27, 30
fab haddie and gooey egg	*72*, *73*
fried	28
melting eggy-bread sandwich	29

F

fritters, corn	145

G

ginger	
ginger chicken with cocnut rice	114, *115*
joy soy lamb and ginger rice	*136*, 137
guacamole	64, 108
gumbo, wicked wild fish	71

H

haddock	71, 75
chile-lemon-splashed fish	86, *87*
fab haddie and gooey egg	*72*, *73*
ham	
chile-jam ham steaks	145
prosciutto turkey roulades	122, *123*
smoked	81
sunny-side hash 'n' ham	28
honey	70
honeyed tarragon quick chick salad	*38*, *39*

L

lamb	

jazz and spice shepherd's pie 138, *139*
joy soy lamb and ginger rice *136*, 137
lazy luscious lamb biryani *132*, 133
snappy lamb hot pot 134, *135*
spiced shish skewers *130*, 131
leek pan pizza, saucy salmon and 74
lemon 70
   chile-lemon-splashed fish 86, *87*
   citrus banana soufflé omelet 185
   citrus-crusted cod with cajun spuds 88
   garlic butter sole with citrus mash 90
   lemon caramel strawberry nests 168, *169*
   zapped lemon curd dessert 179

M

mango 183
   amazing mango marzipan tartlets 175
   mango cranberry nut crumble *176*, 177
marzipan tartlets, amazing mango 175
meatballs
   marvelous chile-cheese
      meatballs *150*, 151
   turkey dumplings with spicy broth 99
mincemeat 164
mushroom risotto, medley of *48*, 49
mussels, wicked wine-steamed *76*, 77
mustard basil beef rolls 158

N

noodles 118
   Canton stir-fried beef with noodles 141
   doodle spinach 'n' chicken
      noodle *112*, 113
   tossed beansprout shrimp noodle *78*, 79
   yum yum nutty noodles *54*, 55

O

omelet
   cheesy cherry tom potato *26*, 27
   citrus banana soufflé 185
onion
   cheese 'n' onion tarte tatin *44*, 45
   rings 155
orange
   chocolate-orange drizzle fruit *172*, *173*
   Silvana's orange tagliatelle
      suzette *188*, 189

P

paella, simply smokin' *80*, 81
pancakes, Chinese-style 125
pasta 151
   admired avocado salsa *68*, 69
   bubbling webbed-cheese 52
   corta spini-chile 53
   cream bean dream 148, *149*
   Pavarotti 152, *153*
   spaghetti mount pesto 61
pasties, Clare's chile bean ranch *20*, *21*
pastry
   phyllo 46, 174

puff 20, 175
   plain pastry 45
pears 164
pickles 92
pies
   jazz and spice shepherd's pie 138, *139*
   rocky road potato cod 89
   scrunched spiced apple cream pie 174
pizzas
   saucy salmon and leek pan pizza 74
   Silvana's pan-fried pizza italiana *50*, *51*
pork
   broiled peppery pork and apple 140
   double-quick Caroline's cassoulet 156
   French-style pork with
      root purée *146*, 147
   Joe's bake and glaze
      sticky ribs 142, *143*
   spice brit's pork chop chow 144
potatoes
   caramelized tuna 22
   Cawley's classic fish and chips 92, 93
   citrus mash, with garlic butter sole 90
   crispy batton bacon potato cakes 23
   crunch lunch cod and *84*, 85
   galettes 161
   garlic 144
   honeyed 104
   omelet, cheesy cherry tom *26*, 27
   parboiled 134
   rocky road potato cod 89
   root purée, French-style
      pork with *146*, 147
   salad, Peppy's posh *40*, 41
   stuffed 19
   wedges 155
prunes 147
purées
   butter bean 97
   root 147
   tomato 71, 100

R

rhubarb 186
rice 133
   golden sunglazed apricot rice *166*, 167
   lamb and ginger rice *136*, 137
   medley of mushroom risotto *48*, 49
   pilau 110
rigatoni 53
risotto, medley of mushroom *48*, 49
rosemary chicken, Mozzarella-oozing 98

S

saffron 81
salads
   honeyed tarragon quick chick 38, *39*
   Peppy's posh potato *40*, 41
salami 41
salmon 71
   flashed smoked salmon bagels 30, *31*

saucy salmon and leek pan pizza 74
salsas
   admired avocado salsa pasta *68*, 69
   cod kebabs with Aztec salsa 82, *83*
sandwich, melting eggy-bread 29
sausages 104
   my Maddie's spicy *154*, 155
shrimp 81, 89
   tossed beansprout shrimp noodle *78*, 79
   chips 17
smoothie, Sydney's fruit coconut *170*, 171
sole with citrus mash, garlic butter 90
soups
   chicken and corn *16*, 17
   clam chowder with Parmesan croutons 18
spaghetti 148, 151
   mount pesto 61
spinach 49, 53
   and blue cheese tart *46*, 47
   doodle spinach 'n' chicken
      noodle *112*, 113
spring greens 49
squash stew, speckled-eye 60
strawberry nests, lemon caramel 168, *169*
suzette, Silvana's orange tagliatelle *188*, 189

T

tagliatelle 82
tarragon quick chick salad, honeyed 38, *39*
tarts
   amazing mango marzipan tartlets 175
   cheese 'n' onion tarte tatin *44*, 45
   spinach and blue cheese *46*, 47
titillating tarty rhuby souflette 186, *187*
toffee-choc cake pudding, terrific 178
tomatoes 22
   cheesy cherry tom potato omelet *26*, 27
   ketchup 70
   purée 71, 100
   sauce 50
tortilla chips 107
tortillas
   "arriba" speedy gonzales 64
   cha-cha-cha chimichangas 108, *109*
   guadiana tortilla olé 65
   mighty Mexican tortilla cheesecake 62, *63*
tuna
   caramelized tuna tatties 22
   golden tuna fish triangles 70
turkey
   chiang mai thai bolognese *120*, 121
   prosciutto turkey roulades 122, *123*
   teasing turkey pitta pockets 36
   turkey dumplings with spicy broth 99

V

vegetables, tingling Thai-spiced 56, *57*

W

wine, dry white 76, 147

acknowledgements

A big thank you goes to Silvana Franco for testing
the recipes along with Bridget Colvin and Annalisa
Aldridge; also to Angela Nilsen at *Good Food
Magazine* for her early inspiration whilst I created
the recipes; to my producer Caroline Officer and
assistant producer Orla Broderick for all their hard
work, energy and enthusiasm; to my researcher
Sarah Williams (what a cracking job).

Thanks also to Bazal Productions and all at BBC
television and BBC Books, especially my editor
Nicky Copeland; to my agent 'Come on the Blues'
Jerry Hicks, Sarah Dolkin and, of course, to my
delightful wife Clare and our adorable kids Jimmy
and Madeleine.